LIVING THE
CELIBATE LIFE

LIVING THE CELIBATE LIFE

A SEARCH FOR MODELS AND MEANING

A. W. Richard Sipe

Liguori/Triumph
LIGUORI, MISSOURI

Imprimi Potest: Richard Thibodeau, C.Ss.R., Provincial, Denver Province, The Redemptorists

Published by Liguori/Triumph, an imprint of Liguori Publications, Liguori, Missouri • *www.liguori.org*

Library of Congress Cataloging-in-Publication Data

Sipe, A. W. Richard, 1932–
    Living the celibate life : a search for models and meaning / A. W. Richard Sipe ; foreword by Francis M. O'Connor.—1st ed.
      p. cm.
    ISBN 0-7648-1098-7
    1. Celibacy—Catholic Church. 2. Catholic Church—Clergy—Sexual behavior. 3. Catholic Church—Doctrines. I. Title.

BV4390.S465 2004
248.4'7—dc22   2004057719

Printed in the United States of America
08 07 06 05 04   5 4 3 2 1
First edition

To Sister Rose Alice Althoff, O.S.B.
and
all the nuns and priests
who taught me about
living a celibate life

CONTENTS

PART III
THE PRACTICAL LIFE 119

FOREWORD

When my friend, Richard Sipe, was preparing his first book, *A Secret World: Sexuality and the Search for Celibacy* (Brunner/Mazel, 1990), I invited him to lecture to a class in theology at a Jesuit college where I was an instructor. Most of the students in the course were in their senior year in the college. "Celibacy in the Church" was to be the topic of the lecture I had proposed. Celibacy was not exactly a hot topic for these young people.

That was in 1990, and when I announced the subject the student response was one of puzzlement and incredulity: "Ho hum," "So what?" Little did they realize what they would learn about celibacy in that one-hour class with our guest lecturer. At the end of the semester, student evaluations of the whole course rated Richard Sipe's single lecture on "Celibacy in the Church" as a highlight of the course. If I were to invite him now, all these many years later, to appear before another class to address the same subject, I have no doubt that our guest lecturer would receive a warm welcome and even more enthusiastic praise from college or university student listeners.

During the years that have intervened, Sipe has continued his research and refined his understanding and passion for the subject of celibacy. Today he stands as arguably the most careful, compassionate, and preeminent spokesperson on celibacy as a way of life. Undoubtedly, he is an expert devoted to every aspect of celibate practice. His name is indeed a household word for those reflective people interested in that subject. Were the late German theologian, Bernard Häring, to comment on this present volume, he might well exceed the praise he offered on Richard Sipe's earlier book, *Celibacy: A Way of Loving, Living, and Serving* (Liguori, 1996), which Father Häring described as "the best of all books on celibacy." Readers of this present work on celibacy will notice that its author continues to search for the true meaning and role of celibacy in the same spirit of honesty, courage, and prayer as he did in his previous writings.

While he maintains a deep respect for the tradition and practice of celibacy in the Catholic Church, he challenges the automatic identification of celibacy with the Catholic priesthood. Rather, he reaches out beyond the confines of Catholic clergy and illustrates the practice of celibacy by many others who are not members of the clergy and indeed are not members of the Catholic Church.

The reading audience to which this volume is directed is somewhat surprising. The book keeps one eye on people "on the inside" who are trying to live a celibate way of life. But it also has in its line of vision others "on the outside" who, for their own various reasons, are considering celibacy as a way of life or who wish to understand the true meaning of celibacy for their own purposes. These groups could include members of communities of religious women, the many laypeople who live exemplary lives of celibacy, individuals who are not members of the clergy but who are celibate, who may want to be celibate, or members of the laity for whom this issue is one of current interest.

This is a workbook. It contains a series of questions and challenges that invite readers to face honestly, and to accept comfortably, their own sexuality. Chapters offer guidelines to encourage a practical search for the meaning of celibacy and to its personal relevance to a way of life. To guide us along the way, the author, in effect, puts a human face on the institution of celibacy. He offers us real people—some ancient, some contemporary—who have embraced celibacy whether in the Catholic clerical tradition or not.

These historical models include Jesus himself, the apostles, saints Paul, Antony, Augustine, and contemporaries like Thomas Merton, Henri J. M. Nouwen, Mahatma Gandhi, and Dorothy Day. It is comforting to recognize in some of these celibate models a pattern of struggle, occasional compromises, and even failures in the process of coming to terms with their personal achievement of celibacy.

One reader or another who has engaged in the process of celibacy may well recognize in the historical models some of her or his own experience in the search. I personally am one of those readers who feels my own experience articulated and clarified here and there in their stories. This means that I have used the book in one of the ways intended by the author—as a workbook. He says the primary aim of every subject in the book is to be a mirror. "The reflection one is after is a clear and accurate image of oneself—a realistic reflection. The reader is the only one who can provide that."

My own personal experience of the celibate life fits easily into the definition of the author. Sipe's definition was accepted into *The Oxford Companion to Christian Thought* (Oxford University Press, 2000): "Celibacy is (1) a freely chosen, (2) dynamic state, (3) usually vowed, (4) that involves an honest and sustained attempt, (5) to live without direct sexual gratification, (6) in order to productively serve others, (7) for a spiritual motive."

The book invites its readers to reflect on each of these numbered elements as they use this book. The historical models of the celibate life put flesh on the elements of the definition and make the definition come to life.

The principal focus of this book is on the choice of a celibate way of life, but it also presents the choice of marriage as a natural alternative. Marriage and celibacy are both presented as ways of life that are good. They both offer happiness, fulfillment, service, and sanctification. Neither one is exalted nor denigrated at the expense of the other. Each way is a freely chosen way of loving, living, and serving. Each is a gift that is a calling, a vocation. Celibacy is described as a friend, and the reader concludes that celibacy and marriage are themselves friends. They are different but complementary ways of being.

The achievement of celibacy—the incarnation of Richard Sipe's definition—does not happen overnight. It is a process in which a person freely forms a clear intention to be celibate. The intention or choice is formed with the confidence that the celibate life is indeed desirable, possible, and achievable. It is usually—but not always—a vowed commitment for life. The intention does not deny one's sexuality but views this important part of human life as a beautiful creation of God.

The Christian celibate's motive is a personal love of Christ and others through him that develops and deepens in time. This personal love of Christ and the celibacy associated with it offer freedom to serve others in love. Celibacy is therefore service-oriented. Celibacy is rightfully "for others." It frees people to be available for loving service. This availability for serving others implies therefore that celibacy is achieved in community with humanity in large or small groups.

Celibacy being a gift and a vocation given by God, one has to pay attention to the situation of homosexually oriented women and men. Homosexuality is of necessity a major concern for Catholic theology and ministry. A larger proportion of homosexually oriented men have always been among the ranks of the Catholic clergy— saints, popes, cardinals, bishops, and priests—than are represented in the general population. Richard Sipe gives full attention to this area of human nature in his book *Celibacy in Crisis* (Routledge, 2003).

It is clear that he cannot agree with the often-heard statement that "it doesn't make any difference if a priest has a homosexual orientation; he's a celibate." Everyone's celibacy builds on, and embraces, one's sexual nature. Sipe's major thesis is that grace builds on nature. He also clearly rejects the unfortunate wording of some official Church statements wherein a homosexual person has been described as "intrinsically disordered." He finds no basis in the nature of human sexuality to justify such a judgment. Nor does he feel those statements reflect accurately the Church's thoughtful theological attitude about homosexual people, celibate or not.

At this point, the Catholic Church does maintain that homosexual orientation is not in itself sinful, but it teaches that the homosexual person is inclined to an "intrinsic evil." It maintains that all deliberate homosexual activity is sinful. This stance is a misrepresentation. Science, theology, and pastoral reality will never be satisfied with this level of distortion of God-given nature.

Sipe's dedication to the pursuit of a clear, honest, and reasonable understanding and practice of celibacy arises out of his conviction that celibacy well lived will bless humanity and this will lead to an enhanced appreciation of sexuality, marriage, and Christian life. As Catholic teaching now stands, every thought word, desire, and action outside of marriage is mortally sinful: every sexual act within marriage not open to procreation is mortally sinful; this standard is a celibate standard. The majority of Catholics do not believe, or follow, this teaching. Thoughtful Christians are unable to accept this standard for themselves or their children. The *sensus fidelium* rejects this reasoning. Celibates should glory in this standard for themselves as their chosen way to live and love. Others cannot.

Homosexuals, within and outside the ranks of the Catholic clergy, are the standard-bearers for a more rational discussion of all aspects of human sexuality, because they cannot silently disregard Church teaching as the majority of Christians do. They are commanded to avoid sexual activity with each other; this is fine for dedicated celibates. Are others to accept an obligatory celibacy? Are gay and lesbian people who cannot honestly claim that they have the gift or a vocation to celibacy to reject their nature—themselves?

What, then, is to be said about the Church's teaching that celibacy is a gift from God? How can this compute with the stance that gay and lesbian people must avoid homosexual activity because it is sinful and therefore they must be celibate? The Church cannot reasonably presume that homosexuals—or any other Christians—have the gift of celibacy and a call to it. Nothing in nature supports this. This area of the Church's life is one that is waiting for further realistic and honest reflection. Men and women who are leading a genuinely celibate life, not merely pretending, have a leadership role cut out for them.

Sipe says confidently, from his years of study and professional experience, that to be celibate one must sustain daily awareness and commitment. "Celibacy has to be proved on a daily basis—primarily to oneself." It is a gift that must be integrated into one's daily life. He touches on some areas and attitudes that challenge that integration: work, service, success, failure, relationships, and love.

How might this integration take place in an ongoing way? As a Jesuit priest who is trying to fulfill the author's rich definition of celibacy as presented in this book, I make a prayer each day that

Saint Ignatius Loyola, founder of the Society of Jesus, considered to be the most important daily prayer in his life. The effectiveness of this prayer is not limited to Jesuits, or priests, or men and women religious. It is eminently suited, but not limited, to those who want to live celibacy.

In Latin, the prayer is called the *Examen.** It is much richer than an examination of conscience. It is more appropriately called a "Consciousness Examen." Father Dennis Hamm has explored it as a way of "Rummaging for God: Praying Backward Through Your Day."** This is a way I like to pray, because it forces me to face God where I find him in my day's experience. There is no need to look for prayer material. Our own experiences are always there for use in our prayer.

The *Examen* takes about fifteen minutes each day. I offer a description of this Consciousness Examen as a way of looking prayerfully and honestly every day at my celibate experience intermingled with other experiences of that day. I try to integrate the reflection on my celibacy with the daily consideration of work and associations. Where am I today? Where have I found God's active presence in the rest of my life? I, like many Jesuits, prefer to use this prayer twice a day, although some say that once a day is sufficient to sustain them. Ignatius of Loyola taught that if a Jesuit—for whatever reasons—can make only one prayer a day, the *Examen* should be the indispensable one.

The *Examen* is divided into five steps:

1. *Prayer for Enlightenment:* I ask God's Spirit for guidance to see myself as God sees me. This request is really asking for honesty and truth about myself. Related to celibacy, I might simply pray for God's light to shine on my celibate life today in order to see it through God's eyes.
2. *Thanksgiving:* Here I recall God's gifts to me today; name them; be grateful for them; they are all signs of God's love for me. Among

---

* George Aschenbrenner, S.J. *Consciousness Examen: Updated Version.* Jesuit Center, Wernersville, PA, 2000.
** Dennis Hamm, S.J. "Rummaging for God: Praying Backward Through Your Day," *America* (May 14, 1994).

those gifts might be my ongoing commitment to live the celibate way and the freedom I receive with this gift to serve others lovingly.

3. *Review or Reflection on the Day:* What or who was in my heart today? What movements do I not want in my interior? Did I notice God present in those movements and in my other experiences, in people I met? Where did I find God? Was I faithful to God's invitations, including God's ongoing invitation to celibacy?

4. *Sorrow:* An expression of contrition is appropriate if I recall any compromises or infidelities or selfishness. I strive for self-awareness that makes former lessons available to warn me of dangerous trends that might be developing. I also remember God's loving mercy for me.

5. *What About Tomorrow?* I look at the future, embodied in the day ahead. I am optimistic and confident that God's loving presence will sustain me as I continue to accept his invitations, including the call to celibacy and the opportunity to serve others in love and freedom. I pray here to be lovingly available to God and to others in my celibate life. I pray to find God in all things because God truly lives in all things.

This prayer can be adapted to fit each person's needs and prayer life. If celibacy is a gift, then the *Examen* is one way of saying "thank you" for that gift. If celibacy involves a process or is part of one's daily life, then the daily *Examen* puts one in touch regularly with the quality of one's commitment to celibacy. It is a useful reality check that places us in direct contact with the God of all reality.

Finally, as a Jesuit, I suggest to the readers of Richard Sipe's book a prayer that was a favorite of Father Pedro Arrupe, S.J., a late and beloved superior general of the Society of Jesus. Celibacy is founded on love. I hope that this prayer may strengthen that foundation in the readers of this book. I offer it to you with love.

Nothing is more practical than finding God.
That is to say: than falling in love
in a quite absolute, final way.
What you are in love with,
what seizes your imagination,
will affect everything.
It will decide what will get you
out of bed in the morning,
what you will do with your evenings,
how you spend your weekends,
what you read,
who you know,
what breaks your heart and
what amazes you with joy and gratitude.
Fall in Love.
Stay in Love.
It will decide everything.

FRANCIS M. O'CONNOR, S.J.

INTRODUCTION

S ome years ago I wrote *Celibacy: A Way of Loving, Living, and Serving* (Liguori, 1996). It was based on over thirty years of reading, reflection, and the experience of counseling hundreds of celibate-seeking men and women, plus an ethnographic study of the subject. I am going to trust the judgment of Bernard Häring when he said that it was by far "the best of all the books on celibacy" that he had read "and the most helpful." He added, "For a long time, it will be the classic on this important question."

I hope he is correct.

This book is not a sequel. In fact, it is a prequel, if you will indulge my use of cinema slang. The scandal and public exposure of sexual abuse by clergy so prominent in the press and legal arena since 2002 forced me to revisit the subject of celibacy to see what I had missed in my understanding the first time around.

The current scandal is centered on only a small percentage of priests who are non-celibate in a most destructive way. But the spotlight of exposure could not be restricted to individuals or a single mode of celibate violation. The whole subject of celibacy and the range of celibate failure on all levels of clerical life, including abuses of clerical power, have come up for review. It is a bit like pulling a loose thread in a knitted sweater. There is no place to stop. Once it became clear in the popular mind that some priests who claim to be celibate are not in fact, where do the questions end?

Although brutal and painful, a public examination of conscience about celibacy is not simply a negative undertaking. A great deal of good can result from this crisis, for celibates and married folks alike. Clarity and truth are surer guides to life than secrecy and deceit. They are indispensable for any spiritual life.

The crisis has not shaken my regard for the tradition and the practice of celibacy. Nor has the crisis diminished my admiration for all the noble people I know who embrace celibacy as a way of living, loving, and serving. It has led me, however, to ask, "What did I miss?" And I have come up with some insights.

First, priesthood is the logical place, as I had always assumed, to examine celibacy, but seminaries are not the best places to look for it.

Second, celibacy that is supposed to be a prerequisite for ordination to the priesthood is not in current practice a real condition for that sacrament. Seminarians, even if they are sexually abstinent for more or less extended periods of time, are too new to the process of celibacy to be called "celibates." I have written extensively on the process of celibacy that has essential phases (*A Secret World*, Brunner/Mazel, 1990). Seminarians and young priests may or may not have strong and sincere intentions to be celibate. That and abstinence is but an initial untried step.

Experience and current observation confirms that there is indeed a great deal of sexual activity that goes on in modern seminaries on the part of students and some faculty. Saint Peter Damian already in his eleventh-century *Book of Gomorrah* decried the commonplace practice of spiritual advisors having sexual relations with those in their care. This practice persists along with a good deal of sexual experimentation between students.

Third, the Church is insistent on the law of celibacy for all priests and religious, but it has been very indulgent—in reality, neglectful—with cardinals, bishops, and priests who do not practice celibacy. I am not referring to those priests and religious who are involved in a "sustained attempt" to be celibate, but struggle from time to time with daunting temptation. Rather, I speak of those members of the hierarchy who sustain long-term sexual relationships or patterns of involvement contrary to what they stand for and preach.

Fourth, and most importantly, I discovered that celibacy is a vocation in itself. The practice is subject to undue pressure and failure if it is adjunctive rather than primary to one's life adjustment. In short, the false identification of the popular assumption that "priest equals celibacy" has left unexamined the dynamic of celibacy as a lived reality and therefore crippled even more the efforts of those who wish to live it.

The lives of some of the world's most treasured saints have a lot to teach us in this regard. Saint Francis of Assisi, for instance, was never ordained a priest and only became a deacon at the end of his life and by the insistence of some of his disciples. His dedication to celibacy was fundamental to his life, and his conversion from what he called his "wild and senseless youth" was a conversion to celibacy and not to the clerical state. His life commission to "heal Christ's Church" that was "in ruins" was not a priestly authorization but a personal commitment in which we can see the raw and essential power of celibate vocation.

I have scores of books on celibacy in my library and have consulted scores of others. They teach a great deal, but almost without exception they start all their expositions from the vantage point of grace. I have learned that spiritual words and premature theologizing can actually conceal rather than reveal the true meaning of a spiritual reality.

Nowhere are physical realities more primary in any spiritual consideration than in the study of celibacy. Grace does build on nature. Nature cannot be shortchanged in regard to celibacy without severe peril to individuals and any institution that wishes to garner its power.

My approach in no way denigrates the spiritual or dismisses the power of prayer or the necessity of grace. But these resources will never replace the obligation we have to use reason to rightfully appeal in prayer for grace to complement or complete the nature we offer for enhancement. We develop from nature to grace, and that is how I intend to proceed in this volume.

PART I

WHO WILL SHOW THE WAY?

Wisdom is not communicable.
The wisdom that a wise man tries to communicate
always sounds foolish.

HERMANN HESSE, *SIDDHARTHA*

The thrust of this work is not to offer someone else's understanding of celibacy, but to help the reader find his or her own. This is not a book of answers. It is book of questions. It is not a collection of directions. It is a series of reflections that offers bits and pieces that will become nothing unless the reader puts them together.

I intend this work to be more practical and personal than theoretical—directed at people who want to consider the possibility of celibacy as a way of life, who may want to take stock of the state of their celibate progress, or who may wish to discern something of the real nature of celibacy as a point of understanding. I also hope it will interest some folk who are looking for a glimpse of celibacy from the inside.

All our considerations start from the point of view of the natural—the stuff upon which grace builds. That "stuff" is the genetic, biological, psychological predisposition, and the intellectual capacities that form a person's unique birthright endowment. Also primary consideration is given to the *natural law* properly so called. That is: "The law based on the innate moral feeling or the inherent sense of right and wrong held to characterize human beings" (Webster). Our starting point is human nature and reason—informed reason open to grace. This point of view is purposeful and deliberate. Also, celibacy is looked at as a primary vocation just as marriage is. Perhaps, in the beginning, our approach will seem confusing to the reader who expects celibacy to be put into a spiritual context and to function as a subsidiary of a "religious" vocation. But decades of study, observations, and sharing with people who have pursued celibacy as a vocation have taught me to think again—to revisit—celibacy as a way of living, loving, and serving.

Spiritual and idealistic treatments about celibacy are not hard to find. They are difficult to follow in practice—in realistic terms—unless one has a solid foundation in nature. That foundation is characterized and solidified by the acceptance of who one really is, stripped of all moralistic denials and spiritual rationalizations. In this process, one presents himself or herself spiritually naked, undefended by gloss or pretense. At least, this conclusion is one that arises out of my experience of fifty years.

Love, service, and sacrifice are beautiful words. Sex, sensuality, and lust are often seen as frightening words. Celibacy involves them all in action.

Who will lead the way through the maze—verbal and actual— toward your goal of celibacy? No one. The issues of love and lust, sex and abstinence—all must be dealt with on an individual basis. This book aims to help unveil the hidden nature of sexuality and celibacy as it applies to the individual person.

1

A CELIBACY KALEIDOSCOPE: SHIFTING UNDERSTANDINGS

Insofar as theologians fail to take account of physics and biology, their interpretations of their own data as well as their models of God must inevitably lose credibility.

CHRISTOPHER MOONEY, S.J.

When I was a seventh-grade student, the assignment to make a kaleidoscope was the one I enjoyed the most. I imagine that the teacher's rationale was to teach us something about optics, color, illusion, and machines. She was clever enough to find a fascinating learning task that would keep us quiet. It was fun.

But even more it was a challenge to learn by doing. While building a kaleidoscope was fun, it was also challenging. It was an opportunity to put some theoretical stuff into practice—to make an idea real and to develop a sense of mastery.

And—that is what this book is all about.

At first glance celibacy—sexual abstinence—might seem a simple and straightforward topic with clear-cut boundaries. All the pieces seem to be easy to find, easy to talk about. Hundreds of men and women easily seem to have put it all together. Anybody can do it.

Nothing could be further from reality. All the questions, controversies, emotional eruptions, and political pressures that surround the study of other human sexual behaviors also beset and bedevil any serious exploration of sexual abstinence.

Although temporary or periodic sexual abstinence is a common human experience, even that topic is not easily broached. Those who wish to incorporate long periods of meaningful celibacy (for example, celibate periods that are not the result of external forces or emotional fluctuations) into their life adjustment have few places to turn for effective support, validated experiential models, and a coherent understanding of celibate/sexual development.

The fundamental challenges to an understanding of celibacy stem from three sources: the nature of human sexuality; religious teaching about sex; and—surprisingly—from the long-established rule of celibacy within the Roman Catholic priesthood and religious life. Assumptions from each of these areas throw down a unique series of gauntlets in front of anyone seeking a deeper and more balanced understanding of sexual abstinence.

The sexual drive—with its feelings, desires, and responses—is such a fundamental part of human nature that a noted biologist was led to exclaim, "Celibacy is the greatest sexual perversion!" But sexual nature is far grander than just its drive. Sex is involved with embodiment—part and parcel of being human. Each person must come to terms with his or her individual sexual nature, whether one chooses to be sexually active or to be celibate.

Every society, to a greater or lesser extent, imposes some limits on the three fundamentals of power: property, sexuality, and myth. Every Church pronouncement on celibacy since the Council of Elvira in A.D. 309 has included consideration of these elements. Bishops, priests, and deacons were forbidden to have sex even if they were married. This was partly to protect church property from being dispersed to a cleric's children and family. Sexual violations, especially by clergy were severely punished by long periods of fasting, public penance, excommunication, and even deprivation of the sacraments at the time of death. The Council sanctioned a wide range of sexual violations even by clergy and included sexual abuse of minor boys. Some sexual violations were equated with heresy, the rejection of orthodox belief. Homosexuality was considered not simply a sin, but a heresy well into the sixteenth century. Many religious traditions glorify virginity and celibate dedication, teach and treasure chastity, and foster sexual restraint. Religions throughout the world are deeply invested in their particular views on sex. Christianity has made moral and political power the linchpins of its fight to preserve and foster certain customs and standards of sexual behavior. Even today the sexual agenda of the Church is paramount in the struggle for control and conformity. The Church is active and explicit in its teaching on abortion, contraception, homosexuality, masturbation, the use of condoms, sex before marriage or after divorce, mandated celibacy for priests, the exclusion of women from ordination to the priesthood. In the minds of many Catholics, these issues should be open for discussion. Currently, the Church holds that these are closed, settled topics and violation of its proscriptions or even dissent involves serious sin. Consequently, sexual transgressions often engender deep-seated feelings of shame and guilt. Religion fosters control through this guilt, and at times has instigated and led or, at the very least, supported societal sanctions against those behaviors regarded as "deviant."

Roman Catholic Church law demands celibacy and "perfect and perpetual chastity" as a condition of ordination to the priesthood. The essence of this religious obligation brooks no compromise. The Church is explicit that religious celibacy takes special grace to sustain it. It is a charism. At the same time, this standard of sexual abstinence is imposed on any single Catholic. The law leaves no room for sexual experimentation, developmental experiences, transient or long-term sexual relationships.

Not many expect that the average single Catholic abides by this standard, even if they maintain it as an ideal. Priests and religious, on the other hand, are presumed to be living by this law and standard. This longstanding tradition, with its absolute parameters and limited population, makes priests a fertile resource for the study of celibacy. (There are approximately four hundred thousand priests worldwide; and forty-three thousand in the United States.)

Few priests and other religious disclose their celibate/sexual struggles in writing; there are some exceptions, even among modern autobiographers, where the writer explains his views on the practice.

However, even a writer as forthcoming as Saint Augustine leaves readers to puzzle out for themselves great areas of the mind and heart of a celibate.

Sexuality in general—and celibacy in particular—are far too complex to be easily divined: They inhere on too many human levels, from the biological to the psychosocial. Even when a person is sincerely reporting his or her own sexual/celibate behaviors and accommodations, it is still not always easy to construct an accurate picture of the whole. These layers of memories and meanings take considerable work to understand and require substantial care to decipher—even under the best of circumstances.

In reality, a whole range of sexual activities has been recorded in the lives of some who call themselves "celibate." Portrayals of celibate ideals and transgressions in modern novels, cinema, and the press also contribute to discourse on the ideal as opposed to the reality of celibacy.

Of course, religiously motivated celibacy is not just about sex—its presence or absence. It is also about love, relationships, service to others, and personal integration. A commitment to celibacy is one way of coming to terms with oneself as a sexual being.

Celibacy originates in cultural traditions, in religion, in nature. The primary challenge to having a dialogue about celibacy, regardless of its origin, is to define precise terms that allow mutual understanding. The steps to achieve this definitional precision necessitate putting together facts and fragments of ideas from many sources. These will result in clearly defined concepts—terms for a dialogue—that accurately synthesize the variety of perspectives. The end product will be an integrated whole that reflects the multifaceted, ever-evolving, meaningful role celibacy plays in human life.

The ideal of celibacy as a worthy goal is not compromised by the acknowledgment of the often less-than-perfect factual reality of its practice. The two can coexist. But first there must be honesty.

We need to be able to accept a definition of celibacy that reflects reality—fact and experience—rather than exclusively insisting on a view of celibacy as we would have it be—rooted in idealization, wishful thinking, and denial. We need a lived celibacy that is an accurate reflection of the person who practices it. How else can we ever hope to come to terms with the kaleidoscopic variations of human nature, imprecisely reflected in celibacy?

The material in these chapters is of secondary importance. The reader's reflection on, and assessment of, himself or herself is the essential element and purpose of this book. It is a workbook, in the sense that it presents a chance to work through the issues surrounding the concept of celibacy. The primary aim of every topic presented here is to be a mirror. The reflection one is after is a clear and accurate image of oneself—a realistic reflection. The reader is the only one who can provide that.

For several centuries, the seminary system provided a structure and discipline that was designed to promote and inculcate celibacy and enhance intellectual life among candidates for the priesthood. The development of the seminary system from the time of the Protestant Reformation onward was a leap forward in the education of clergy. However, even the most balanced and well-developed programs were not always successful. And, what was practicable within seminary walls was not always able to be translated into pastoral life.

The seminary system is increasingly inadequate to meet the task of promoting celibacy. In 2004, a major seminary in Austria came to international attention when forty thousand pornographic images were found on the school's computers. Also photographs of students and faculty fondling and French kissing were exposed. The local bishop dismissed the incidents as "boyish pranks" and minimized the evidence as a "traditional New Year's" exchange of greeting. Lay Catholics and those outside the influence of clericalism do not respond lightly to such behavior.

I do not intend this book to be in any way a negative commentary on the current practice of celibacy. Rather, I desire to use my experience and knowledge as a useful companion to anyone who wants to think seriously about the celibate process in a personal way. But I am obliged to acknowledge that behavior like this is far more common within the seminary system than anyone would like to admit. Some seminary faculty and even bishops have inappropriate and sexual relationships with students.

In attempting to address the sexual abuse crisis that has gained international attention, the hierarchy has repeatedly focused on increased attention to the selection of candidates for the ministry. That may be part of the problem, but the core of the problem of sexual violation by clergy abides deep within the clerical system and at exalted levels. The problem of sex abuse of minors by clergy is as old as the Church and can be traced in church documents. Successful church reforms, and there have been many throughout the centuries, always touched the *system* of the Church, that is, its inner operation. Every reform movement has also had to address sexual violations by clerics.

I was a student in Rome, at an international college, during the 1950s. The European students who had had to interrupt their theological studies to fulfill their country's military service requirement impressed me. During two years of military service, they were "on their own." They were not set apart as special—they were just men.

There was a particular—and real—quality to their understanding of celibacy, quite distinct from some students who had been trained in a seminary setting exclusively from their early years onward. I have maintained contact with several of these men for a period of fifty years. They have taught me a lot about the celibate process and commitment. I owe them.

But you could say that my perspective is the result of many years of trial and error—even failure—in teaching courses on celibacy to eager theologians. I entered my last classroom venture in 1996 with great enthusiasm. After years of teaching, I felt I had all the right elements—a class of twelve students who claimed they wanted to be celibate, three full weeks devoted to this seminar alone, and a world class bibliotherapist to conduct daily group-sharing sessions. I had my daily lectures prepared. The only other requirement was that each student spend an hour in private "reflecting" on the day's "material."

When the seminar was finished and the evaluations in, not one student had spent the time in private consideration. When questioned, as a group they said that they understood the presentations, and so concluded, "what was there to think about?" They had missed the point, because I had missed the point.

The first part of this book is titled "Who Will Show the Way?" The short answer is "no one." We will talk more about this need for personal responsibility as we progress. Celibacy is not viewed merely an academic subject for one who wishes to practice it. It is profoundly, intimately, and even dauntingly personal. This personal approach is imperative because celibacy is wrapped up with individual identity, individual sexuality, individual relationships, and individual adjustment to life itself. Part of this struggle cannot be shared. Part of it cannot be learned. It cannot be justified or hidden beneath idealistic imagery and even genuine piety. The process of celibacy has to be a lived experience. It has to be the person as he or she really is. Celibacy has to be a clear and realistic reflection of an integrated individual.

2

CHARTING A COURSE:
DIFFERENT PERSPECTIVES

Our first task is to become fully human.

THOMAS MERTON, O.C.S.O.

A fter saying that this is a personal guide to a work in progress and not a text, I may seem to be going back on my word as I digress to a brief reminder of the history of celibacy. Be patient. You will see that this material forms a foundation for future consideration.

Celibacy is generally understood as a state of nonmarriage and/ or abstinence from sexual activity. Confusion results if religious celibacy is limited to this definition since one can be unmarried but sexually active or married and sexually abstinent. Christian celibacy demands greater specificity. It presumes a lived reality.

Here is the definition I use: Celibacy is (1) a freely chosen (2) dynamic state (3) usually vowed (4) that involves an honest and sustained attempt (5) to live without direct sexual gratification (6) in order to serve others productively (7) for a spiritual motive.

In a concentrated fashion, we will reflect on each of these elements as we go along and consider as well the other mirrors history puts before us. For instance, Christian tradition assumes that Jesus Christ was not married, but there is no clear testimony to his singleness in the gospels. There is an ancient, but minor, tradition that

Jesus was married. It is useless to argue that either speculation is absolutely and incontrovertibly established. For our purposes, it is more productive to leave the question open just as the Bible does.

Customarily, Jesus' comment about being a eunuch for the sake of the kingdom has been used as scriptural support for clerical celibacy, but more current studies relate these words to their context of marriage and divorce (Mt 19:10–12).

Paul talks about his personal choice of celibate dedication in his epistles where he also commends temporary sexual abstinence for married couples who want to devote themselves to a period of prayer. He also cautions the married and single to remain in their current state, but his reasoning was conditioned by his thought that the end of the world was near (1 Cor 7:7–8).

Some Catholic scholars argue that all the apostles were celibate after Pentecost, but this position is in direct contradiction to Paul's claim that he had a right to a wife just like the other apostles. The standards for bishops that he enumerates in his other epistles clearly indicate he is talking about married men (1 Tim 3:1–7).

The history of celibacy has been skewed by the relatively modern emphasis (since 1546) of celibacy as a clerical prerogative. Actually women and nonclerics played a monumental role in the development of celibacy as a way of life. It was hermits and monks who developed the most defined theory and practice of celibacy as a mode of spiritual awareness and devotion in the early Christian centuries. Celibate women were a significant force in perpetuating and purifying the tradition; their history goes largely unacknowledged.

John Cassian (360–435 A.D.) in his *Conferences* reflects the most astute and enduring analysis of the nature and meaning of religious celibacy. His explorations confront directly the inextricable relationship between human sexuality and celibacy. He was the premier exponent of the celibate process. He traced the progress from sexual restraint to a total transformation of sexual activity on all levels of internal desire and expression. He taught that contemplation, fasting, study, and divine grace are indispensable for the practice of religious celibacy.

The practice of celibacy did not begin with Christians. Already in

529 B.C. Pythagoras established a community of celibate philosophers who devoted themselves to intellectual and scholarly pursuits.
Other Platonic and Stoic philosophers held that teachers ideally ought
not to be married. That tradition held in medieval universities even
when the professor was not a priest. Christian writers were emphatic
that the ideal, motivations, and dynamics for Christian celibacy were
distinct from those of the philosophers.

The shared natural and psychological roots of the urge to be celibate have been underestimated. In both lines of development, some
proponents applauded celibacy at the same time as they were denigrating marriage and demonizing women. Needless to say, disregard-
ing nature and denigrating either sex is a shaky foundation for celibate living.

Early Christian writers extolled celibacy as a mythopoetic equivalent of martyrdom. The admiration for religious celibacy is grounded
in its witness of a gospel love so encompassing that one is willing to
sacrifice anything or everything in the service of others.

Without doubt, the asceticism and spirituality recorded in Christian lives and literature has its center in celibate love as a preeminent
way of imitating Jesus and dealing with human sexuality. Religious
celibacy has been a durable mode of spiritual witness, insight, and
dedicated service. Millennia of Buddhist, Hindu, and Christian practice have proven the force of this discipline.

The first and second centuries of Christianity were centered in
family and homes. Sexual righteousness was a consideration for laity and presbyters alike, but celibate practice was not formalized.
The roles of priest and bishop evolved slowly. As clerical power grew
during the third and fourth centuries, an ever-clearer split developed
between the laity and clergy.

At that time, hot debates ensued about whether or not celibacy
should be required of priests as a mark of unalloyed dedication and
proof of a spirituality worthy of wielding ecclesiastical power and
service. In fact, these concerns were recorded in every church discussion of clerical celibacy. I have already mentioned the very first written record of a church synod (Elvira, A.D. 309) that imposed a requirement of sexual abstinence on its deacons, priests, and bishops,

married or not. Every council throughout history that looked at clerical celibacy has been concerned with three things—procreation, property, and power—and these beyond any and every spiritual or ascetical dimension. The logic of this concern is that sex leads to children who by inheritance will disburse church property and, at the same time, marriage is diffusing the control of a bishop over his priests.

Among others the Lateran Councils (1123, 1139, 1179, and 1215) as well as the Council of Trent (1545–63) echoed the concerns of Elvira for establishing and preserving control over church property (condemning simony, the sale of church goods), sexuality (ruling marriages by clerics invalid), and power (asserting church law above secular control).

The Council of Elvira also gave witness to the extent of sexual problems among the fourth-century community. Thirty-eight of the eighty-one canons regulate sexuality and consider sexual transgressions by laity and clergy. Very severe punishments were dictated for bishops, priests, and deacons who transgressed sexually, the higher the office receiving the more severe censure. Those who abused boys were among the most excoriated.

The first ecumenical Council of Nicaea in A.D. 325 debated the question of obligatory celibacy for clerics. The ideal had already forged strong bonds with the priesthood, but even the celibates present argued convincingly against mandatory regulations. The debates about the requirement of celibacy for priesthood have always been peppered with fierce attacks on those clerics who professed it, but disregarded it in practice.

Saint Peter Damian wrote the *Book of Gomorrah* in 1051 and presented it to Pope Leo IX. In it, Peter reports on the widespread sexual immorality of clergy and the lax enforcement of celibacy by religious superiors.

In 1568, Pope Pius V updated the legislation of the Lateran Councils in his document *Horrendum*. He emphasized the gravity of clerical soliciting sex with men, women, and young boys.

Throughout history, many popes, bishops, and most priests were married until Rome promulgated universal legislation for the Latin

Rite during the Second Lateran Council in 1139. For all practical purposes, questions about a married priesthood were ruled out of existence when the Church declared invalid any marriages of ordained men. Married men could no longer be ordained. Legislation, however, did not end the sexual activity of priests and bishops—nor of all popes.

The Eastern Christian church had settled the question of clerical celibacy for itself at the Council of Trullo in A.D. 691 by declaring that bishops must be unmarried and sexually abstinent. Married men can be ordained priests; single men who present themselves for ordination, however, must agree to remain unmarried and abstinent.

The Protestant reformers relied more on the biblical foundations of Christian ministry than tradition and believed that the medieval insistence on clerical celibacy was wrong and corrupt. The question of an unmarried versus a married clergy became a litmus test for both Protestants and Roman Catholics. Catholic orthodoxy required belief in the Real Presence in the Eucharist, celibacy for its ministers, and submission to the authority and supremacy of the pope. Protestant Christians judged that it was a good thing for clergy to marry and rejected papal claims to authority.

By far the greatest opprobrium leveled against religious celibacy throughout the centuries has been aroused by those who profess to be celibate but whose behavior turns out to be neither celibate nor religious. Sexual failures of clergy that involve hypocrisy and violation of truth are a perennial concern.

Twenty-first century men and women are being exposed to clerical corruption similar to that found at the time of the sixteenth-century reformation. A sense of crisis surrounds questions of human sexuality, mandated celibacy, and church authority.

The reality of religious celibacy is far more significant than debates of mandatory or optional celibacy for Catholic priests. These debates will be settled in time. Celibacy is a gift to humanity and will endure throughout the ages, but can it be legislated? Our concern here is not legislation, but free choice. Celibacy should be available and supported wherever it is inspired in any Christian. Celibate dedication can offer insight into spiritual reality and provide a human service that is inestimable. Gandhi wrote that any nation is poor without such persons.

Naturally, the Catholic priesthood lends itself to study for the purpose of understanding celibacy, not because it has a monopoly on the interest or practice, but because celibacy is a prerequisite for Catholic ordination. And, in fact, the alliance of celibacy—a way of coming to terms with one's sexuality—has been so closely identified and even subsumed under the rubric of "priesthood" that the identity of celibacy has been distorted and imperiled even for priests.

Understanding this close identification has solved a puzzle—one I have wondered about intently for a long time. Priests called "celibates" can write ecstatically about the ideal of celibate love and life. But these same men, explicitly and professionally dedicated to a celibate identity, have great difficulty describing their celibacy in practical terms from their life experience. Sex and celibacy are difficult to talk about in real-life terms.

The list of canonized saints is long. Priests and martyrs head the list, along with virgins and a few widows. No married person with an ordinary marital life has yet entered the ranks. A married couple who Pope John Paul II proposes for sainthood practiced celibacy for the final forty-six years of their marriage. The Church has not yet developed a theology of sexuality refined enough to include sexual activity into the realm of perfection. On the other hand, there is a long history of celibate failure on the part of those who publicly professed celibate dedication.

Certainly, throughout the Christian ages, some married folks have attained sanctity by means of the fullness of their married love. The undue emphasis on sexual abstinence as a means to Christian love does a disservice to marriage. But, more importantly, it distorts the idea and practice of celibacy.

First, undue emphasis on sexual abstinence as a means to Christian love promotes the myth that celibacy is a "higher" way of life than marriage. The Council of Trent did hold that celibacy was a higher state. Vatican II seems to counter the anathema that Trent imposed on anyone who held the states were equal. Celibacy is neither higher nor lower than marriage. It is a valid way to love and serve, when it is the right way for a woman or a man.

The second myth is that celibacy makes someone special and entitled. Not so. If celibacy is the right way for me, it is simply that—my way. But it does not endow one with special prerogatives.

Confusion about celibacy leads people to think that it is some kind of automatic, "holy" condition that makes a person's personality and behaviors above reproach and unquestionable. Some have called it a "state of perfection." This nomenclature sets the stage for the cover-up of real transgressions that would damage the image of near perfection in regard to sex. This need to propagate and preserve "image" has been at the bottom of the current crisis that involves sexual abuse of minors. Celibacy is not, and never should be, an empty moniker that cloaks and justifies moral compromise.

These distortions indicate the importance of revisiting the whole area of sex, celibacy, and marriage. Sanctity should be open to every Christian, and both avenues—marriage and celibacy—should be a viable means to holiness. When reflecting realistically on celibacy, we must never forget that charity and truth, not chastity, are at the center of Christian morality.

Facts demonstrate that many priests—good, hardworking men—do not succeed very well in the practice or achievement of celibacy. At best, they are deprived of the particular rewards of this life adjustment and the consolation and gratification that mastery alone can crown. At worst, they can be driven to a life of self-deception and perversion. And in between there is a host of people who suffer too much and needlessly struggle too hard.

Why? I will venture an answer. Because although celibacy is legally a prerequisite for ordination in the Latin rite of the Catholic Church, in practice it is not revered as the separate and distinct vocation that it is. Celibacy in the priesthood has become an adjunct and consequence of ordination rather than a real prerequisite.

The promise to be celibate for a lifetime is made just before a man is ordained to the deaconate. The commitment is part of the ordination ceremony, and it is certainly a beautiful part of the ritual. The bishop says:

> By your own free choice you seek to enter the order of deacons. You shall exercise this ministry in the celibate state, for celibacy is both a sign and a motive of pastoral charity, and a special source of spiritual fruitfulness in the world. By living in this state with total dedication, moved by a sincere love for Christ the Lord, you are consecrated to him in a new and special way. By this consecration you will adhere more easily to Christ with an undivided heart; you will be more freely at the service of God and mankind, and you will be more untrammeled in the ministry of Christian conversion and rebirth. By your life and character you will give witness to your brothers and sisters in faith that God must be loved above all else, and that it is he whom you serve in others.

The bishop then asks the candidate directly:

> In the presence of God and the Church, are you resolved, as a sign of your interior dedication to Christ, to remain celibate for the sake of the kingdom and in lifelong service to God and mankind?

Once the candidate answers "I am," the ordination ceremony continues. Is the man really ready to commit to lifelong celibacy, or is he only prepared to become a cleric? The ceremony is an additional stamp that presents priesthood and celibacy as one entity rather than two independent and separate—no matter how interrelated—physical, psychological, intellectual, and spiritual processes and commitments.

I taught in major seminaries for over a quarter of a century. Many men expressed doubts prior to ordination to the priesthood, not about priesthood, but about celibacy. Some, when they sought advice from

seminary officials were reassured that they had normal "preordina-
tion jitters." Others were told that "after ordination" everything
would fall into place. The uncertainty can be so great that literally
on the eve of priesthood ordination a deacon can say, "I don't know
that I want to sleep alone all my life."

My teaching experience holds wonderful memories of witness-
ing the growth and development of young people toward their
goals. But it became ever clearer as the years went on, when I
was able to talk to former students and interview other priests,
that something was basically missing in preparing men for ordination. Because celibate preparation was assumed, no real training was offered. "Celibacy" was considered to be the necessary
byproduct of seminary training, when clearly it is not. It cannot
be.

Celibacy is a unique process, not a derivative of a seminary system. Law and ritual pose celibacy as a prerequisite for ordination,
but in reality seminaries do not respect, train for, or test as if it were
true that attaining a celibate life is a unique process.

I was puzzled for a long time why so many priests failed at celibacy when they were successful in so many other aspects of their
lives and ministry. I have been impressed with the number of priests
who leave the priesthood after many years of service. I have been
concerned with the limited number of men entering priesthood and
religious life. Noted researchers have said that vocations to the priesthood would increase fourfold if celibacy were not a requirement (cf.
Dean Hoge, *The Future of Catholic Leadership: Responses to the
Priest Shortage*, Washington, D.C., 1987).

A prerequisite is precisely that: something required before one
can move on to some other task or gain admission to another level
of education or employment. We all know that we have to complete
high school to enter college, pass the MCAT to apply to a medical
school, the LSAT to apply to law school, and so on. However interrelated, high school, college, and professional training involves distinct tasks and levels of achievement.

Or think about other sets of prerequisites. An airplane pilot must
have a certain standard of vision in order to be trained and licensed.

A U.S. Marine must meet basic physical requirements before qualifying for training.

If celibacy is to be a genuine part of priesthood, it has to be treated seriously as a quality that is present prior to ordination. For those who wish to be celibate in conjunction with some other mode of work or service, it will be clear that celibacy is a vocation—one worth striving for.

I came late to the insight of just how significant it is to understand celibacy as a distinct vocation. I "knew" canon law said that celibacy was required—a prerequisite—for ordination, not a result of a sacrament, but it did not register that in practice that stance was disregarded. Celibacy was conceptually so bound up with the priesthood that a "priest" became synonymous with a "celibate." Of course, this equivalence is not an operational reality.

Unless celibacy is, in fact, treated as a vocation in itself, educated for as a vocation in itself, judged as an achievement in itself, it will fail in the service of the priesthood or any other venture.

I have never entered into the hot-topic polemic of a married priesthood versus a celibate priesthood. This book, as everything else I have ever written, can be used in the service of discussion on both sides of the issue. But it is historically clear that marriage is not intrinsically opposed to priesthood. Other rites than the Latin one have consistently ordained married men.

Celibacy is not intrinsic to priesthood. Priesthood is not intrinsically oppositional to marriage. There is a solid tradition of celibate practice that can be traced to Gospel times, explicitly in the testimony of Saint Paul. But there is just as strong a tradition of married Christian service, even among the apostles. This tradition of married and celibate disciples (laypeople, apostles, priests, bishops, and popes) continued in the Latin rite for a thousand years.

There are witnesses of married priests in Orthodox Christianity; they share the same apostolic tradition as the Roman rite. And even

Rome has accepted certain Anglican and Lutheran married ministers for ordination.

But celibacy is intrinsically distinct from marriage. Each is a particular way of relating to self, others, God, and the world. Each is a special and distinct way of channeling sexual energies. Each is a way of loving and serving.

Celibacy and marriage are distinct from our work and service relationships. One can be a married scientist or a celibate scientist, a married physician or a celibate physician. One can be a married or celibate artist, politician, or scientist. The trials, struggles, demands, and rewards of each sexual adjustment and way of life are distinct and in many ways unique. But both are compatible and can be supportive of any work or profession.

Certainly a person's sexual adjustment and integration will influence all aspects of life, love, and service at some fundamental level. But this influence is as true of marriage as it is of celibacy.

It is a fact that Pope John Paul II has spoken decisively about the requirement of celibacy for ordination in the Latin rite. These reflections do not enter into any argument with his judgment. Quite the contrary: this perspective emphasizes the importance of respecting celibacy as a prerequisite for ordination as a Catholic priest, not merely an accretion to priesthood—no matter how intimately the two are bound.

Celibacy is not a spiritual monopoly of men or clergy. It is open to women and men in equal measure—open to laypeople as well as religious. It is the "right" way for many people. Many people fail to consider it as a possibility for themselves.

When celibacy is examined as a distinct vocation—rather than as a prerequisite for ordination to the priesthood—the real nature and beauty of the vocation becomes apparent. Anyone who would like to understand the phenomenon of celibacy or anyone who wants to consider pursuing it as a way of life will do well to think of it as a durable vocation in itself. It can't hurt.

3

CELIBACY AS A POSSIBILITY

You would rather throw stones at a mirror?
I am your mirror, and here are the stones.

RUMI

Those who see celibacy as a possibility for themselves should look into the mirror of their intentions. What is seen in this reflection? Is celibacy deeply desired? Why? Note that no one can answer such questions right off or definitively at first consideration.

Perhaps the thought of celibacy came slowly, or suddenly, or on the heels of some life event that changed the perception of life, such as a significant death or separation? I have known men who endured war, women who have lost a husband, people who have survived a life-threatening illness, or others who have faced the vacuousness of the failed self-indulgence they had hoped would bring them happiness. Each came to embrace celibacy as a friend.

The life of John Henry Cardinal Newman is a fascinating tale of celibate commitment. He was sixteen years old when he determined that he would lead a celibate life. And he followed through for a lifetime. Anglican at the time, there was no other vocational pressure on him to influence his decision. There are men and women who know at a relatively young age that they, by choice, will never marry. From my vantage of seventy years, I can say I have known people who should not have married. They missed their celibate vocation.

Asian spirituality and societies revere celibacy. Hinduism holds the celibate ideal in high esteem, but it is not in any way connected with priesthood. Buddhism has a long tradition of dedicated celibate practice—lifelong for monks and nuns. In fact, its origins were identified with the practice that was considered necessary to attain enlightenment; to live as Buddha lived.

Monasteries accepted disciples from a very young age, but perpetual celibacy is not the only practice accepted in candidates. The average believer can join a community for shorter periods of time. A year of celibate practice is common among devout believers. As religion evolved, even a tradition of married Buddhist monks developed.

The Asian view of the life cycle and attainment of meaning remains distinct from the European tradition. Asia is more in touch with nature, including sexual nature. Youthful sexuality and parenting are considered the normal path to meaning and spirituality. Sex and spirit are not oppositional, but rather part of the pattern that leads quite naturally to greater levels of contemplation and celibate practice. Wisdom, celibacy, and old age are seen as the culmination of a life well lived.

Religion and spirituality are not the only motivations for celibacy. As I said earlier, philosophers like Pythagoras, Apollonius, and Epictetus taught that the best teacher was one who was unmarried. The motivation for this prerequisite was to allow the teacher to make a more substantial contribution to society. These thinkers were all pre-Christian. The earliest Greek community of intellectual scholars was established six centuries before the birth of Christ. This tradition—that a dedicated scholar should be single even if he was not a cleric—extended well into the Renaissance. Elizabeth Abbot published her *A History of Celibacy* in 2000 (Scribner). She does not restrict herself to a religious definition of celibacy, but casts a wide lens on professional characters, historical and contemporary, who chose not to marry. She includes Leonardo Di Vinci, Isaac Newton, Florence Nightingale, and so on, among others who may or may not have been sexually active. Even today, some men and women dedicate themselves to celibacy because their art, or science, or devotion to an extended family, or particular cause fits with a celibate lifestyle.

Men and women, sexually active or not, can come to a realization that they have a celibate vocation at any time in life. Even priests and nuns who have identified themselves as "celibate" to themselves and to the world for a long period of time can come to the realization that their sexual adjustment is neither religious nor celibate. Amazing as it seems, when they looked closely into the mirror of their intentions, they saw clearly that they never really "intended" to be celibate. They kept their intentions vague and undefined. They drifted and hid behind an image only to discover that they were, and wanted to be, a sexually active person.

Some priests and religious recognize even before they take vows or make the promise of celibacy that they are on shaky ground. Although their doubts are substantial, they quiet themselves with easy rationalizations or succumb to facile reassurances, often from well-meaning advisors. Frequently, individuals on the verge of marriage find themselves in a parallel situation. Both life junctures are too important to be superficially dismissed.

Any doubts about a life choice that has significant and long-term repercussions are daunting and should be taken seriously. But the choice of marriage and priesthood are not commensurate. The choice of priesthood or religious life is a double choice, one of work or ministry and a separate one of sexual determination. Who and when one marries are distinct from the work one chooses.

Confusion and defective support frequently arise out of the failure to appreciate the fact that the moment of promise or vows is an elision of two separate vocations. The vocation to be a priest is not identical with the intention to be a celibate person. Just as the vocation to celibacy is not identical with the intention to be a priest. They can be intimately related, but they are separate and distinct physical, psychological, and spiritual processes. Usually the ordinary process and pressures of life offer one the opportunity to face one's treasured self-deceptions and the chance to pick up the scattered pieces of one's efforts and missteps, and to clarify the ill-defined intentions.

It is not realistic to think that one can clarify intentions by accident. It takes work. At any temporal juncture a person can clarify his or her resolution and reevaluate the mixture of their celibate intent.

The best intentions rarely are single-minded, unclouded, and uncomplicated. We sometimes want and don't want the same thing simultaneously. Or we want something sometimes or under select circumstances. A common mistake has been made about celibacy, namely, that it is a static state. It has frequently been associated with a state of perfection however one defines that.

No human enters into an unalterable and unchangeable "state" short of death. No doubt, a natural human longing exists for stability, security, and an existence with as few unpleasant surprises as possible. But that is only relatively possible whether one is sexually active or celibate. To be human is to change. And as Cardinal Newman said, "To be perfect is to have changed often." And no matter the combination of elements one finds in the reflection of her or his initial intentions to be celibate, evolution is inevitable. Human beings will change, clarify, and refine their intent as they experiment with the idea and ideal. The practice of celibacy cannot become real until you bring all the jagged, multicolored, contradictory pieces of one's kaleidoscope of intentions into focus.

I advise those considering celibacy to be sure to look more closely into the mirror of their intentions especially if at first they see only positive motives. Love, service, and the "will of God" may all very well play a large part in the intention to be celibate. But a person practices self-deception if he or she thinks these motives are unalloyed and completely refined at the beginning of the journey.

Fear is a common human component in human motivation. In the end, of course, fear becomes stultifying—inhibiting growth. But it has been said that fear is the beginning of wisdom. The wonderful thing about searching our motivations and intentions is that we can use all the raw materials we find—no matter how gross and unrefined—to produce purer and more sophisticated spiritual selves. Truth is the one condition of transformation of fear into wisdom.

It is tough to admit that we might be afraid of intimate relationships, of sex, of family responsibilities, of competition, or of a dozen other more idiosyncratic boogeymen we can carry from childhood. But if these hidden forces are in an undeveloped person, there is no way to avoid them and their consequences forever. Eventually, they will surface and trip up the unsuspecting if they are allowed to remain hidden. On the other hand, don't expect to uncover these hidden forces all at once. That's not possible. We give up our secrets to ourselves slowly. Of greatest importance is the desire to know our real intentions, whatever they may be.

Everyone is motivated to a degree by self-preservation. Some women and men see a safer, surer way of life as a single and celibate person. This vocation is where they feel sure of themselves and in control. Celibacy can be a person's space for self-protection. Persons with a vocation to marriage can have the same fears as others, but they don't feel sure, safe, or in control as a single or sexually abstinent person.

Celibacy is a means of coming to grips with sexuality, just as marriage is in its own way. Both are "selfish" in the sense that they are justly and rightly for ourselves and as a means to a fuller life for us. Each way of life is meant to provide a distinct source of satisfaction and sense of selfhood and mastery. Granted, either marriage or celibacy can be neurotically and even pathologically self-serving and narcissistic. The best of intentions can be corrupted, but that does not diminish the inherent possibility for good that both sexual solutions offer.

Sexuality is not an end in itself, whether one chooses to be a celibate or a partner in marriage. Sex is a necessary part of our nature. Our task is to incorporate it into our lives as part of a reality greater than ourselves—our love and our work. Which sexual adjustment is an individual's means to a fuller life? Which is the best vehicle to develop an individual's talents, service to others, fulfillment of the capacity to love? Is this choice "right for me?"

That question will not be answered to anyone's satisfaction without repeatedly asking it. One ancient tradition holds that celibate intention must be faced and renewed every day. That makes so much sense. If celibacy is dependent on a special grace—a charism dependent on a Higher Power—it should not be presumed on any basis other than "one day at a time." That is how grace is meted out.

What a person contemplating celibacy needs to consider above all is his or her freedom. You cannot be free in your choices unless you look squarely at your intentions. We will talk more about this need to freely examine your intentions when we consider the step from the intention to be celibate to making the vow to be celibate.

4

WHO IS THIS PERSON CONTEMPLATING CELIBACY?

Everyone is a moon and has a dark side
Which he never shows to anybody.

SAMUEL CLEMENS

When anyone is asked "Who are you?" we have standard responses that make us look good. We highlight our assets, emphasize our solid origins, breeding, education, and experience. We identify ourselves with our profession; we indicate values that we hope will establish a bond with the inquirer. It is only natural to want to make a positive impression.

It becomes quite a different question when no one is around—when we are the only one involved in the question and answer. "Who am I?"—If I am honest, I can't impress myself. I can only fool myself. The challenge of looking into the mirror of our souls is daunting. It is frightening. The quest for the answer is lifelong. But we have to start sometime, and it is advisable, if possible, to begin the search before we decide on a vocation.

Granted, self-knowledge is the height of wisdom. "Know thyself" the Greek oracle said. It all sounds too simple to have much meaning or to keep our attention for very long. The trouble is that it is too enormous a quest to be achieved lightly, easily, or quickly. Like all grand quests the hard part is getting and staying on the correct path. There are myriad delightful distractions to keep one from concentrating on the journey.

A major, constant problem of knowing oneself is that the phenomenon is like looking into a magic mirror—we can see exactly and only what we want to see. The more serious the pursuit, the more the mirror metamorphoses into the likeness of a funhouse glass—everything is distorted. Of course, the real distortion is not in the glass, but in the viewer in us. Most of us don't want a really clear picture of who we are.

We have to expect pain in the process of working out all the ugly little urges and tendencies that "are" us. All the sufferings, abandonments, insults, losses, disappointments, rejections, and sadnesses of growing leave traces on the landscape of our being. The pattern of erosion coexists with the flowers and foliage of love and nurturance we received along with our sense of mastery and accomplishments. How to sort it out?

Oscar Wilde sketched a dramatic metaphor in his *Portrait of Dorian Grey*. The main character remains youthful and vibrant looking as his portrait ages not only physically but also graphically, revealingly tracing his true moral status which is one of ugliness and decay. The outward image and the interior reality are in opposition and at odds. The true image of the Church and the face of the priesthood should be a living icon of Christ. The integrity of the Church has been repeatedly challenged throughout history. Pretense and hypocrisy distort the image of priesthood and Church far beyond offending individuals. The sexual abuse crisis in the Catholic Church has brought many believers to seek the true identity of the Church beyond its image, good and bad. The cost of keeping up appearances rather than truthful self-acceptance is disastrous personally and corporately.

We are all faced with the challenge of incorporating the elements of our history and character into a coherent whole so that our true self is reasonably consistent with the image we present. That is what "who I am" is all about. Anyone contemplating and discussing the capacity to commit to celibacy will have to face a deeper level of self-examination, but even in an initial exploration it is a significant requirement.

We discover an important part of ourselves as we review our affective life. Who have we loved? What have we loved? How have we loved? Celibacy (like sexuality) is not a way to live out of the deprivation of an affective life, but a way to live out its fullness. When we trace who and how we have been loved and our responses to being loved (and also how we have handled rejection), we will begin to see patterns—some adequate and reasonable and others that we will want to modify.

Our relationships with others—and from our earliest years—can also tell us much about our style of interaction, our strengths, weaknesses, and ourselves. Paying attention to others and how they react to us can show us sides of our personality to which we are blind. Certainly, we should listen to what others have to say. Advice from a trustworthy friend should always be welcomed, but even then it should be accepted with a critical ear.

A lifetime of experience compels me to add a word of caution to those embarking on a quest for self-knowledge in regard to gurus—any gurus. During the last century, psychotherapy, counseling, and spiritual direction have inundated and saturated our society. Newspapers and magazines are full of advice columns. Television's most popular programs involve "true confession" and free advice. Advice-giving is a multibillion-dollar industry. We have become so accustomed to turn to someone else for answers to personal questions that we have lost touch with the reality that, in the end, we must answer—and indeed are the only ones who *can* answer—the question of who I am.

Another caution must be given in regard to a reality called transference and countertransference that becomes operative whenever two people get together and share intimate thoughts and feelings. There is always an unrealistic element in every transference relationship. The transference bond can range anywhere from simple admiration to overdependence and beyond to a frankly pathological distortion.

One reason this caution is important is the most obvious. If one is going to pursue the possibility of living celibacy, he or she must deal on a deep level with his or her sexuality which is always an emotionally charged area. Self-examination and exposure make a person vulnerable. But that same vulnerability extends to any advisor whose own sexuality may not have been adequately explored and who thus may seek to act out those repressed feelings with the person seeking advice. In addition, celibacy is a lonely, necessarily a solitary, commitment. That essential loneliness can set a person up to be a victim of sexual boundary violations. Empathy can be translated into physical affection. As the psychological professions have matured, awareness has increased of the significant proportion of advisors, from psychiatrists to priests, who impose their own unresolved problems on the people who come to them for understanding.

The real tradition of spiritual guidance was established on the solid reputations of genuinely holy men and women. The role and the right to dispense this wisdom was not given to everybody and was acknowledged to be special gifts—in the same way that sanctity was recognized as a very special gift.

It is wrongly presumed that every minister should have the capacity to be a spiritual director or guide by virtue of his ordination. This presumption is an extremely dangerous one. The psychological movement of the last century has made the same mistakes about its trained and licensed practitioners. Rigorous training is one safeguard, but by no means does it give the vulnerable all the protection they need against psychic and sexual violation.

When the Fourth Lateran Council established the requirement for individual sacramental confession in 1215, the tradition of selecting a confessor on the basis of his holiness was forever compromised. Like surgery, once a part of the barber's profession, it could not survive with integrity in a mundane form. Thus, persons seeking to discern their celibate vocation or to live a celibate life must seek their advisors and confessors most carefully, with a lot of reflection and due awareness that things are not always as they appear. It is wise not to be trapped by an affective judgment when making such a selection. An extensive search may have to be undertaken for the most suitable and trustworthy advisor.

Personality tests such as the Myers/Briggs, the Enneagram, the

Minnesota Multiphasic Personality Inventory, and so on, have become popular tools to help people know their psychological makeup and style of relating to the world. Just as with therapies, some people find such tools helpful in the process of self-discovery and others do not. Use whatever supports your growth, keeping in mind that these tools are adjunctive to your main resource—which is your own ability to discern the truth about yourself.

No one and no thing can substitute for a personal and reflective self-evaluation. But nearly everyone and everything can be an aid to self-understanding. Georges Bernanos summed up his classic novel, *Diary of a Country Priest,* with the words *Tout est gras.* Those words have been translated both as "grace is everything" and "grace is everywhere."

Both statements are valuable reminders for the celibate who seeks to understand the mystery of "who am I" to take advantage of the grace that is all around us in everyone and everything. But aids, even spiritual help, are not substitutes for one's own capacity for self-evaluation, self-direction, and self-control.

It may be easier to begin a self-evaluation by seeking out responses in areas that are related to your sexual life, but first only in indirect ways.

One useful indirect question involves how you handle stress. Each of us has a range of responses to cope with pressure and tension. Of course, the more flexibility we have, therefore the more adaptability, and the better equipped we are to meet stressful situations. But most of us, at least at first, have a restricted set of reactions. "Fight or Flight" are the classic categories of stress response. Anyone can maintain equanimity when everything is smooth—no pressure. The true test arises when we must react under tension. We all have preferential patterns. To know them is to be able to control them.

Further reflection toward self-knowledge is critical: How do you handle your impulses? When you want something, observe yourself. How impulsive are you? How thoughtful are you? Do you look before you leap? Again each of us has a range of preferential ways to react. Before we can refine ourselves, we must first acknowledge what comes to us automatically.

All life is marked by some disappointment, some losses, some irreversible circumstances, and impossible obstacles. How does a person cope with and find comfort in the wake of pain? In a way, self-comfort requires distracting yourself without undue denial of the pain and compensating for loss without compromising your integrity. Self-comfort is closely allied with our earliest development as sensual beings—sucking thumbs, being held and caressed, infantile masturbation, and generally pleasantries of touch, taste, smell, and sound. As we mature, intellectual achievements—learning, reading, writing, physical, and manual skills—are added to our repertoire of ways to make us feel better. Varied interests and hobbies are a tremendous help in keeping us balanced in the midst of inevitable loss. This is true for everybody. But these auxiliary means of legitimate comfort are indispensable for a person who proposes to forego one of life's major modes of comfort, sexual pleasure.

Anyone who wishes to consider a celibate vocation must review his or her sexual self, not as an abstract or dismembered part of the self—something that one can put aside—but as an integral element to be lived with. Why not turn to a calm review of your sexual experiences? What has happened to you? Our experiences are a part of us.

Some folks think that a review of past sexual experience will form a "temptation." That may well be true, but unless we face those temptations, inclinations, experiences—call them what you will— they cannot be laid to rest peacefully and really become part of the past. They will remain vital and dangerous, armed like land mines to take us unaware and disrupt progress toward the goal.

What we have been exposed to is only one dimension of our experience. What sexual choices have we made? How, when, why, and where? What feelings, besides excitation, were attached to them? Which are still most vibrant in memory? What we are talking about in this instance is a real, practical, calm, sexual inventory.

Our own sexual history tells us a great deal about ourselves. It is a fantasy to suppose that we can approach the decision to be celibate without a sexual history, since a celibate vocation rests on a foundation of adult free choice. One of the most neglected—and therefore explosive—areas of examination is that of sexual curiosity. I have seen a great number of celibate vocations tripped up by belated and twisted attempts to satisfy what at base is normal sexual curiosity.

In this day and age, it is relatively easy to educate oneself—satisfy legitimate curiosity—about human sexuality by reading solid books about sexuality, talking to educated colleagues, and having a set of resources available to provide answers to legitimate questions about human sexuality. Satisfying a proper "need to know" about sex should not be marked by shame and certainly not by secrecy. Sneaking is not a healthy approach to sex. Pornography is so common that some psychologists have branded it a "normal perversion," and most adults have at least glimpsed it. It is not a good source of sex education. If never indulged, it should not be feared like the plague.

What one has seen sexually, and one's reaction to visual stimulation and education, needs to be incorporated into self-awareness and the knowledge of life. The man or woman who is blind to sex does not make the best celibate. One who sees clearly walks more securely in inevitably dangerous territory.

Jesuit John Thomas used to say that a priest should know everything there is to know about sex save experience. That is solid advice for any dedicated celibate. But most people who want to be celibate will come to their decision with some sexual experience. That experience should not be scuttled into the waste bin of "sin" for easy absolution. Its memory should be retained until it is resolved, absorbed, and transcended into one's celibate identity.

This conclusion has arisen from years of study and I will share with you celibate models who demonstrate just that. Your sexual experiences and curiosity will tell you something about your orientation. Beware. Do not jump to easy conclusions. Do not run to quick assumptions for refuge in an acceptable label or duck reality out of fear. Everyone's sexuality is far too complex for easy categorization.

But with honest self-examination you will be able to sort out your sexual orientation. Heterosexual and homosexual are the basic terms used to differentiate sexual orientation, meaning a basic attraction either to same-sex or complementary sexed companions. It is really not so simple in real life, but you will understand how you fit within those guidelines as you accept yourself and embrace your humanness. You cannot be human without your sexuality.

Neither orientation is an impediment or an advantage to one's vocation as a celibate. Celibacy is a challenge to every human being. Certainly, orientation will determine the color as well as the distinction brought to the vocation of celibacy. Each person has his or her own gifts to bring to life and to whatever life work that is chosen to pursue.

It may take some time to determine the strength of your sexual drive since it is variable in most people and ebbs and flows at rather irregular intervals. The drive can be heightened or lessened by health, mood, stress, or circumstance. So it is easy to fool oneself into believing that "I have it made" when all the internal and external supports of one's life are in balance. Awareness of the vagaries of the sexual drive is one reason to highlight the need for impulse control in leading a celibate life. Simple indulgence in sexual activity will not reveal all there is to know about sexuality. Attention to the entire rhythm of life and productivity over time will help to answer satisfactorily the questions about the strength of the sexual drive.

Drives toward food, drink, relaxation, work, and associations are in some sense related to one's basic sexual drive. Pay attention to them, as well. What do they mean in the total scheme of who you are? Do you use—or overuse—substances, persons, places, or things to keep you from making an honest inventory and disguising your sexual drive?

Analyzing these qualities will lead you also to know something about the objects of your sexual excitation. I have seen many celibates confuse themselves and complicate their lives unnecessarily by not knowing the kind of people or objects that excite them sexually. They are taken by surprise and caught off balance because they were unaware of their particular vulnerability.

To know oneself is a daunting assignment. Really it is a lifelong pursuit. But it is a marvelous journey that bestows self-knowledge and, more importantly, offers wisdom about others and all humanity, opening up the universe in its most ultimate meanings.

5

CELIBACY
TAKES PRACTICE

The glory of God is man fully human.

IRENAEUS

The ideal and the practice of religious celibacy have persisted for millennia, individually, and in a number of religious traditions, notably Buddhism, Hinduism, and Roman Catholicism. Why? Because celibacy has an intrinsic value and vitality. Celibacy is useful to civilization and culture. It serves the propagation of the species in collateral and complementary ways. It is a valid way of life. It is an authentic vocation. It persists in the face of ugly times of scandal, attacks, and denigration.

I have always been intrigued by the facts about celibacy: how to define celibacy in practical—real—terms, not just in ideal encomiums. How do those who claim celibacy, in fact, practice it? How does one achieve sexual identity without sexual experience? What is essential in the process of becoming celibate? What is the structure and substance of celibate achievement? These may seem to be academic questions. They may seem unnecessary and even impudent. But they are important—essential—for anyone who is serious about understanding or living celibately.

I have faced all of those questions seriously and for a long period of time. But I do not pretend that my answers or observations can substitute for anyone else's experience. The last two decades have witnessed the spotlights of the media and the legal system focused on sexual abuse, especially of minors, by clergy who were assumed to be celibate. Millions of people are now exposed to the reality that some men who claim celibacy do in fact violate it even in criminal ways.

Following that thin but substantial thread, we can see that the fabric of clerical culture has begun to unravel and reveals some sexual facts beneath the protective covering of a religious mantle. We know that there is something systemically wrong that cannot be reversed or rectified solely through the efforts and example of the multitude of priests who are honestly celibate.

But one silver lining in the dark cloud that hangs over clerical celibacy is the chance to examine more closely just what celibacy is and to learn how to live it more effectively. The emphasis on the "searching for the factual" is crucial to that understanding and life choice. That quest is equally important for those who have a vocation to marriage. Self-knowledge and self-acceptance are the basic building blocks of every relationship. Knowledge of the other is not possible without them. Knowledge (based on facts, not illusion) is an element of love.

Currently, there is a terrible incongruity between sexual teaching and practice. Factual explorations of celibacy have been scant to nonexistent; idealistic literature about celibacy, filled with image, symbol, and myth is abundant.

With the best of intentions, most writings have been propagated to inspire, sustain, and defend chastity and the law of religious celibacy. Similarly, many explorations have been eschewed by mythopoetic doctrines about sex dealing with the ideal as if it were real.

Even more importantly, however, facts about the nature of human sexuality have been avoided. Celibate myth has been fostered to establish a rationale for the presentation of a moral norm and teaching about sexuality for everyone that is celibacy based. Sexual moral norms are all based on the concept of a celibate morality. For instance, the teaching that "every sexual thought, word, desire, and action outside of marriage is mortally sinful" may well be the choice of standard for the dedicated celibate. This teaching is not in accord with the nature of developing human sexuality. Can this, then, be a realistic moral norm for everyone at all times?

The consequence of such logic means that life for most people should be divided into two parts: the first, an unmarried period devoid of all sexual awareness (or filled with the sins of experimentation or worse) and a marriage where sexual activity is permitted and even possibly sanctified. The ideal celibate's life would be one of sexual abstinence and angelic unawareness from the cradle to the grave. Or it could be one of sexual excess followed by repentance, conversion, and then absolute sexual abstinence. Nonetheless, the norm articulated in the *Catechism of the Catholic Church* (§2351–2391 and 2396) renders everyone an inevitable sinner for a part of his or her life. This norm simply does not correspond with the human nature, as we know it or the experience of dedicated Christians.

Most pastors, however, recognize the limitations of the moral laws about sexuality as currently articulated. For instance, most confessors, and indeed the revision of the *Catechism* itself, indicates wide latitude in judging the morality of masturbation. Use of the contraceptive pill is widely accepted as a matter for individual conscience rather than sacramental confession in spite of legal prohibitions. Even abortion in restricted cases where circumstances are cloudy and health of the mother and child are in severe danger receive pastoral compassion and tolerance, even when understanding is limited. Many pastors do not abandon homosexual couples even when the law labels them involved in "intrinsically disordered" behavior.

The essence of sexual sin does not reside in pleasure, but in a violation of reason, responsibility, relationships, and truth. Think about it for a moment. The sin of gluttony, and there is such a thing, is not about the pleasure of eating. It is the unreasonable consumption of food or drink, the irresponsible disregard of one's responsibility to others, and the violation of an honest relationship even with one's self.

Consider the essential core of anger, murder, deception, or any other moral disorder, regardless of any satisfaction that the perpetrator may take in the action, and you will come to see that it is a violation of the right order of reason, responsibility, relationship, and truth. I believe that my thinking is in line with the moral theology of Bernard Häring.

In contrast, the Church's attitude toward sexual sin is one of act orientation. This orientation takes the act of procreation as the core of natural law, and in so doing involves a philosophical definition of nature and law. Currently, the most common Catholic philosophical and moral basis for teaching about human sexuality is based on the "nature" of the sexual act and not on natural law. The complete nature of the sexual act is capable of procreation, divinely sanctioned by the command to increase and multiply. Acts that do not conform to this capacity, such as masturbation, contraception, homosexuality, and so on, are deemed "unnatural" according to this norm. Vatican II expanded the understanding of marital sex to include its capacity for comfort and companionship. But sexual development is not act oriented; it is not philosophically bound. It is nature oriented. It is a developmental process that involves the deepest physical, psychic, and spiritual capacities of what it means to be human. Natural law, as I have pointed out before, is that law of right and wrong inherent in human consciousness. Pope John Paul II has written a great deal about human sexuality (collected in *The Theology of the Body: Human Love in the Divine Plan*, Pauline Books, 1997). He proceeds from a biblical foundation and clings to a "nature of sexual act" in his reflections. Although he makes a great contribution, no one has yet developed a Christian theology of sexuality. That will come.

If the central concern of a person who practices celibacy is a concentration on the negative—avoiding an act of sex—that person will very likely not achieve celibacy. Why? Because these persons will subject themselves to an inevitable self-deception, thinking that if they can rid themselves from the start of any sexual thought, word, desire, or action then they are celibate. Just the opposite is true. Practicing celibacy means—especially in the beginning of this effort— to be able to tolerate, think through, struggle with all sexual thoughts and desires, and to ask and answer the question: What do these sexual thoughts and desires mean for the individual and about him or her?

Many people in the recent decades have turned to psychological theories and treatments to enhance their self-knowledge and to reconcile their drives and their aspirations. When I began my studies in the 1950s, there was a radical conflict between religion and psychiatry. That hostility has devolved over the years to an alliance that can encompass all sorts of frankly absurd therapies. Those are the ones that countenance boundary violations and indulge in acting out fantasy rather than mastering instinct.

There has been a horrific misinterpretation of Freud and his psychoanalytic method. People said it led to libertine behavior, to guiltless violations, especially of sexual norms, blaming parents, rejecting religion, and so on. That certainly is neither the object nor the process of the method. Analysis can only be conducted within the strictest parameters of deprivation. The fantasies that the process encouraged were not for action, but understanding. The whole object of the method was to free the person to know himself or herself on the most profound level—little by little to face the true self—and then to make free, reasoned decisions, without compulsion, free of impulse or fear.

What many people do is to deprive themselves of sex for periods of time; when the pressure becomes too much they "sin," quickly repent, confess, receive absolution, feel relieved with being forgiven only to repeat the same cycle again.

I frequently had a chance to deal with that pattern when I was consulting with folks who wanted to be celibate. The person would say to me, "I tell my confessor the same things I tell you. But he is satisfied that I just tell him; you always want to know 'why'? and 'what does it mean'? You are never satisfied." And of course, I was not satisfied, and I didn't think they should be either. The blind cycle of "restraint-relapse-reform" most of the time morphs into a pattern that makes celibacy a sham. Celibacy, like marriage that is its mirror image, takes practice, fosters self-knowledge, involves the capacity to relate, and the ability to endure deprivation. Neither marriage nor celibacy is sex-act centered. They are relationship-centered or they are not real and enduring. A married person comes to terms with his or her sexuality in one context, the celibate in another.

Celibate deprivation does cause discomfort. It should not be blind. It may involve slips from its goal, but not senseless repetitions of unexamined desires and tendencies. That road leads ultimately to addiction or to a double life.

Those rigid personalities who depend on externals and rules to keep themselves in check, who glory in winning approval of their elders, who are conformers rather than transformers of their inner life and relationships, are also headed for trouble. They expend great energy in avoiding their sexual selves. Their apparent strength and their stiff resolve, so successful for a limited time and in a protected environment, desert them and cannot long stand the test of reality. After all, that is where all of us have to live sooner or later. Rather than tempered steel—strong and flexible—they are like pressure cookers; they appear solid, but they tend to blow rather than adapt.

During the 1950s, military conscription was not suspended for French and Belgium clerical students as it was for Americans. As I mentioned previously, I knew the European theology students who had to interrupt their studies to spend two years in military service. I indicated that I owe this group for helping me understand celibate development and practice. Years later, while serving on the faculty of an American seminary, I was asked to serve on a committee to revise the seminary curriculum. Inspired by the maturity of these man and their in-touchness-with-reality, I made the suggestion that after two years of seminary studies each student would be required to spend two years supporting himself in some secular setting. Not surprisingly, my suggestions were considered impractical. I felt, and still feel, that seminaries are not very good places to train for ministry and even less adequate to prepare for a life of celibacy. Those who objected to a new way of training seminarians could not do much worse by thoughtful experimentation. Ten percent of priests leave the ministry during the first five years after ordination. Twenty-five percent resigned from the priesthood even before the sexual abuse crises surfaced in the 1990s. These priests have kept up contact for fifty years and shared their celibate journey. The years of interrupted study were not a suspension of celibate development, but a valuable time of practice.

After many years of teaching in Catholic seminaries, I am convinced that seminaries need reform to learn and practice celibacy. The atmosphere now is still too artificial. Fear of sex, rather than a healthy interest in it, predominates. Secrecy and shame are the mode of exchange rather than openness and honesty. That is true of the faculty as well as students. I have also observed that consistently about one-fourth of the faculties themselves are not grounded in celibate practice. Many confessors are sexually vulnerable. They are not sufficiently stabilized in their own sexual awareness and control to withstand the feelings that young people struggling with their own identities evoke in them.

When sexually active superiors, presumed to be mature and safe, impose themselves on unwitting beginners in the practice of celibacy, the very atmosphere becomes tainted. Too facile forgiveness of slips and glib indulgence has the same effect. The process is distorted, almost genetically. It gets passed on and duplicated in other lives.

If you want to be celibate, practice. Don't depend on any institution for more than reasonable support. Celibacy has to be a personal quest, an individual achievement. And certainly it is a spiritual process, but not one that prays itself into existence. I consider the Alcoholics Anonymous program a fine model for any person practicing his or her celibacy. First: maintain absolute truth with yourself—no denial, no rationalization, no avoidance. Second: pay daily attention to yourself and your inner life—celibacy, one day at a time, as Buddhist tradition has it. Third: have an open, honest exposure of your history and being with at least one other person. Fourth: keep an ongoing examination of your responsibilities, relationships, and the reasonableness of your choices.

You may say that saints have formulated similar or superior programs for spiritual growth. Indeed. Therein is part of the problem. When spiritual growth is posed as the fundamental and structural basis of a quest, persons can embrace it prematurely and embrace it to avoid or deny their nature. Their spirituality becomes distorted and ironically they sexualize their spirituality rather than sanctifying their sexuality.

One frightening example of sexualization is the theological theory that considers priestly celibacy as a "marriage bond" with the Church. Thus, the celebration of Mass becomes a "marital act." The Eucharist is transmogrified from a banquet into a sexual exchange at least between the priest and the sacrament. An altar becomes the marriage bed. The reasoning proceeds to the point where this marital commitment to the Church renders the sacramental marriage of a priest adulterous. Cardinal Francis Stafford outlined this theological reasoning in detail at the May 1993 International Congress on Celibacy sponsored by the Vatican. Pope John Paul II has also proposed this thinking to defend the necessity of celibacy for the priesthood and the impossibility of changing the requirement of celibacy because of its "nuptial meaning" and essential connection with the Eucharist (*Pastores Dabo Vobis*, 1992).

Priesthood and celibacy are traditionally closely, but not universally, related. Beyond the error of sexualization in the marriage/celibacy theory is the confusion of the vocation of celibacy with the vocation to the priesthood. According to Church law, celibacy is a prerequisite for ordination. Priesthood and celibacy are not identical vocations anymore than marriage and medicine are.

Marriage and celibacy are distinct ways of coming to terms with one's sexuality. Priesthood is an important way of serving; special, to be sure, but it has to take its place among other vocations of service.

The witness of thousands of victims of abuse has made us all agonizingly aware of the consequences of immature men of the cloth who make spiritual displays, but lack a sense of their own and other's sexual nature. Time after time, victims relate how their abuser, whom they trusted to be celibate, told them, "It is God's will that you be here with me," "You are a blessing from God to me." The utter degradation and betrayal of nature and grace is culminated when a priest anoints his victim with his own semen as if his violation were a sacrament.

Nature, our sexual nature, must be understood, respected, and developed in order for us to submit ourselves rationally, responsibly and truthfully to a promise of celibacy. The beginning of the process is the thoughtful consideration of this way of life and the dedication to its practice. It is a daily exercise, dependent on knowledge, learning, self-knowledge, and awareness. Nothing can make it automatic, instantaneous, or miraculous. Celibacy takes time. It takes work. Celibacy needs practice.

6

COMMITMENT TO CELIBACY:
A PERSONAL JOURNEY

*What would happen
If men were faithful
to the ideals of their youth?*

IGNAZIO SILONE

The choices involved in a commitment to marriage or to celibacy are profound. The consequences are long lasting and influence many people in addition to the principles involved. That statement should not sound dire, just serious.

Commitment should get the attention it deserves. Young people today are well aware of the need to prepare for an enduring relationship. Many talk about "the fear to commit." That caution merits some respect. The difference between a casual friendship and the public declaration of intent is a big step. Celibacy is no less a big step. Status from one who is trying out the celibate mantle to one who claims to be "a celibate" has legal, psychological, social, and spiritual implications.

Most of the time sexual behavior is private. We take that for granted even as we live in a culture saturated with sexual themes and images. But we still cherish the idea that sexual activity—at least ours—is really private. And, indeed, most sexual acts are hidden from public view and scrutiny. That is as it should be. When sexual activity that can be legitimate in private is expressed in public it becomes criminal or at least offensive.

Marriage, however, is a public declaration of sexual and social bonding and commitment. Matrimony is celebrated and acknowledged by a change in title and legal status. It confers the "right" to be sexually active. And marriage partners are presumed to have a sexual life. When a woman becomes pregnant she proves that she has "had sex" in some form or other.

Celibacy, when it is declared by entrance into religious life or ordination to the priesthood, is no longer a private matter. It is a pledge of a firm intention to live and love without any sexual expression. It is a public stance, just as marriage, about which people can make reasonable assumptions. A man or woman who bears the title "celibate" should be "sexually safe." That person is presumed to have come to terms with his or her sexuality. The celibate, by definition, is not free, open, or willing to have any sexual exchange. This belief is partially responsible for the prestige and trust rendered to a person who is advertised as celibate.

Any person who professes celibacy, not merely as one practicing in the sense of preparing or trying out, but one who has a firm commitment to a way of living, has a corporate responsibility beyond the personal. At least this responsibility is true of those who belong to religious groups. Ordination to the priesthood requires a candidate to make a promise of "perfect and perpetual chastity" prior to receiving the sacrament. And groups that require celibacy as a condition for inclusion or affiliation also take on the responsibility to assure the public that their members are celibate with all that that implies. One sign of corruption is the rationalization that celibacy means not getting married, but leaves room for unchaste behavior. Not so. Either in law or in rational public assumption.

It is not difficult to understand what a serious commitment celibacy is and why it demands a rigorous training, solid grounding, thoughtful preparation, and earnest practice.

In my experience the celibate commitment has not been taken seriously by Church institutions. Let me go on record with my reservations. Church authority has spoken consistently about the requirement of celibacy as a condition for ordination. Some may debate that issue on theological grounds. Papal statements have said that even the pope does not have the power to abrogate that requirement. I certainly accept the power of the pope. My argument is not with the regulation, but of the neglect of the reality.

In over thirty years of relatively close contact with seminarians and priests, I have met men on the verge of ordination who express deep reserve about celibacy—they doubt their desire for it, the ability to follow it, and even reject the idea. Some have said clearly that they had no intention of living it.

I have had the chance to evaluate a number of men who were less than a year away from ordination. Each was involved in a sexual affair or in behavior that signaled trouble with celibacy. On every occasion where I had the responsibility to make any recommendation to the cleric and his superior about ordination every suggestion to postpone ordination was rejected. The men were prepared to be priests, but they were not prepared to be celibate.

This was my consistent experience as I counseled priests—good, serious, and devoted men. They readily admitted that they had not been taught about celibacy in the same way they had been instructed in biblical and theological disciplines. The United States Bishops commissioned studies on the historical, psychological, and sociological status of American priests. The conclusion of researches was similar: priests said that they were not adequately instructed in celibacy. This deficiency is related to the conclusion that a majority of priests were psychosexually underdeveloped.

I had to be shocked into the awareness of how sadly celibacy was under-appreciated as a vocation. The first shock came in 1975 while teaching a seminary course in my favorite pastoral subject, "The Person of the Priest." The course was constructed to aid the students to "fit" themselves into the priestly role and challenges by considering clerical models in novels. Novels offer the reader real-life experience and establish an emotional connection better than most other literary forms. We took, for example, the sainted priest in Georges Bernanos' *The Diary of a Country Priest*, the lonely pastor in O'Connor's *The Edge of Sadness*, Graham Greene's reluctant martyr, and whiskey priest in *The Power and the Glory*, Pietro Spina/Don Paolo in Ignazio Silone's *Bread and Wine*. (This, by the way, was Dorothy Day's favorite novel, which she read once every year. I have chosen to follow her example.) Short stories by J. F. Power, James Joyce, Nathaniel Hawthorne, and others also came up for discussion.

My hope was to engage the mind and heart of the students in order to find the essence of "priest" within them. One day toward the end of the semester I had what I thought was a bright idea to test their progress. I asked, "What would you do as a priest if you came to an area where there were no churches, parishes, or schools already established?" Three-fourths of the class said that they would not be priests. I had in mind the first disciples sent out two by two to spread the good news. I even had thought of the Mormon missionaries, sent out similarly to untouched territories and countries.

With disappointment I talked to others on the seminary staff. They told me not to worry; they thought it was just a result of immaturity. I couldn't help but think it was part of a rather shallow commitment to their stated vocation.

Later, when I inquired how many would be celibate if it were not for the priesthood not one ventured that he would. That jostled me, but I could not really compute it at the time. In fact, it took me until after 2002 to put it all together.

Celibacy and priesthood are two separate vocations. Certainly, they can be intertwined by law and related in tradition, but they are separate vocations nonetheless. The one is a prerequisite for the other. I had been blinded by the same kind of logic presented to students on the verge of ordination who had doubts about celibacy at the last minute and who were told that once you are ordained every thing will fall into place.

The realization of this distinction of vocations unraveled a mystery for me. How could so many good men defeat themselves and their Church? How could corruption grow and be tolerated on such high levels of ecclesiastical power? Why could no one within the system speak up about obvious abuse? The violations that have come to light are not doctrinal. They are sexual. Indifference to celibacy and secret indulgence were covering for celibate violation.

The importance of "celibacy" for the priesthood has been emphasized interminably, and solemnly reiterated with conviction. But the fight is really about the law of celibacy—the regulation—not the practice. The Church fails to take celibate violation or practice seriously. And for anyone wanting to commit himself or herself to celibacy the task must be about practice, not appearance.

The power of celibacy is in its lived reality, not its name. Two of the most authoritative witnesses to celibacy in my life experience were not priests—Dorothy Day and Mohandas Gandhi. Dorothy Day was a Communist sympathizer in her youth, an advocate of free love and a social activist. When she became pregnant her lover insisted on an abortion, which she refused. The price she paid was rejection by the man she genuinely loved.

Her former political sympathies were metamorphosed by her conversion to Catholicism, her sexual love was transformed into love for the poor, and her activism was energized for a lifelong quest for justice and peace. Day's conversion was to celibacy. Day could describe her longing for the physical comfort and tenderness of her former lover in the midst of her long loneliness. This dedication to celibacy did not eliminate her sexuality, but transformed it.

Similarly, Gandhi's greatest significance as a witness to celibacy is the frankness with which he treats the growing knowledge and experience of achieving celibate practice. He does not shy away from including accounts of his sexual lapses as he recounts his experiments with fasting and physical renunciation and their limits. He tells the tale of his changing and growing appreciation of what it means to achieve celibacy.

Gandhi is explicit about the value of his vow to be celibate. He spent five years in preparation and experimentation before he took his vow. The chronicle of his development is the most valuable and unique in the history of celibate practice. From the time that Gandhi determined the personal importance of celibacy, he records his progress toward the celibate achievement that follows an authentic pattern of celibate development—awareness of capacity, knowledge of the process, practice, and commitment.

How does a person know if it is time to commit/promise/vow

celibacy? You will have taken the time and made the effort to determine your capacity to be celibate. You will know yourself well enough to know the rhythm of your desires, the strength of your drives. You will be comfortable with your gender and sexual identity—your sexual self. You will know how you to react to stress. You will know your potential for relationships, and community, and solitude, your ability to function alone and to work with others. Sex is not a mystery to you. You will have a mastery of your curiosity. Celibacy will be the way you want to live and love.

Celibacy is not an end in itself. It is a means to serve. If celibacy is part of a person's destiny, it can lead to productivity in whatever work chosen. Both before and after Gandhi formulated his intention to be celibate, he longed for some humanitarian work of a permanent nature. He was aware he possessed the capacity for celibacy. The ability to balance the deprivations of personal celibacy enhanced his potential to live a life of service and gave it meaning.

Celibacy is not a desexualization, nor is it a state of asexuality. The person who practices celibacy as a preparation for commitment will already know that celibate practice embraces his or her humanity fully without fear or dissimulation. "I am me. I am celibate" is the mantra. Fear of self or sexuality, ignorance of self or sexuality, compulsion or guilt are contraindicators of a vocation to celibacy and are serious impediments to any vow or commitment.

Celibacy is not antisexual. The well-adjusted celibate person has regard and reverence for married and sexually active persons. A celibate person is part of a minority, and he or she knows it. Each maintains his or her way of life without the need to exaggerate the importance of a personal individual choice. The celibate is not threatened by married colleagues, nor are they objects of envy. The celibate does not have to reassure himself or herself by denigrating those who have chosen other ways to come to terms with sexuality.

Vowed celibacy is a public stance. It really does not tolerate a secret life. A person whose sexual life is secret is not truly celibate. The commitment means that "I am me," and "I am celibate." I am knowledgeable, thoughtful, and sexually safe because my intent and practice is to operate without sexual gratification. In order to make a commitment, one must be reasonably certain that he or she has the experience to take that position.

Does this commitment obviate any imperfection? No. But the pattern and practice of one's dedication must be clear, and any lapse of judgment must be honestly and immediately dealt with. Any sin or violation of celibacy must not become part of a secret system or a double life.

In short, celibacy is a state beyond sexuality. It is not negative. It is not an avoidance of life or responsibilities. Celibacy is a way of life for some people. It holds its own sacrifices and joys, just as does marriage or any other sexual adjustment.

Some people think that one theoretical stance or the other is responsible for sexual virtue or failure. I have not found that case to be so during my lifetime. Doctrinal orthodoxy is no more an assurance of celibate success than theological heterodoxy (or liberalism) is an indication of failure. Celibacy is dependent on personal qualities of adaptation, flexibility, and loving dedication that have little to do with abstract paradigms or factional politics, no matter how religiously impressed.

One is ready to make a commitment to celibacy when one has knowingly examined his or her sexual potential, sufficiently practiced celibacy, and freely chooses without reservation to embrace a celibate way of life.

PART II

CELIBATE MODELS

Teach thy tongue to say "I do not know"
And thou shalt progress.

TALMUD

W hen it comes to matters sexual, there are historical, scientific, political, and personal limitations that affect everyone. A brief review of select celibate models can help us sort out the essence of the practice from misunderstandings, passing trends, and misrepresentations. The Church law that has decreed that celibacy is essential to priesthood has ironically but, in fact, rendered the practice of celibacy incidental in reality.

The idea of "celibacy" has become so identified with the Catholic priesthood that it has become falsely synonymous with that sacrament. Religious women who have always outnumbered clergy have been largely overlooked as a source of knowledge of celibate practice. This book does not right that wrong, but it may cure some clerical myopia by setting one record straight. The real practice of religious celibacy predated and outstripped the development of clerical celibacy.

Christ and the Apostles are special cases and we will deal with those particularities in their vignettes that follow in this part. But consider other models. Origen vowed celibacy long before he was ordained in Palestine where he had to seek special permission for the sacrament. Anthony was never ordained. All of his ecclesiastical power came from his celibate life alone. Cassian was primarily a celibate monk who sought ordination midway in his career, and his choice was influenced by political circumstance.

Augustine is well known for his conversion. That conversion was a personal conversion to celibacy. He was pressured into service as a bishop. Benedict, the great monastic rule-writer, was never ordained. Francis was likewise never ordained a priest, but tradition has it that he became a deacon.

Among our modern models, Thomas Merton was ordained a priest, but that was the determination of his abbot. He entered the Trappist monastery to be a celibate monk. Henri Nouwen is like so many modern priests who desire the priesthood from their youngest years. Celibacy is successfully embraced as part of that vocation.

Salient to my argument is the fact that celibacy is and has been a unique and separate vocation, no matter how closely allied at times with the priestly vocation. The more celibacy is respected for its intrinsic and unique value, the more easily and effectively it can be lived in reality.

7

Jesus: The Universal Model

This world is the abode of God.
And Jesus truly lives here
And in us.

ANONYMOUS

Jesus is a mirror. Each person can enter into his or her own consideration on what sex and celibacy means in terms of "Who Jesus is for me?" "How do I see myself in him?"

There is a common misconception that Jesus is a more apt and complete model for a celibate—and a male—than for other people. Or put another way, there is a false assumption that a celibate male is the only accurate reflection of Christ. This is not true. Jesus is a model for everyone: woman, man, single, married, and celibate. To hold otherwise is to miss the real meaning of the Incarnation.

The Word-Made-Flesh can be—and is meant to be—heard by everyone equally. There is truly a mystery to the Christian understanding that we are all one; there is no longer Jew or Greek, male or female, slave or free, in Jesus Christ's account.

I recall a young priest who said, "I know that God loves me more than others because he gave me a superior brain." Indeed, he was intellectually brilliant. Humble or logical he was not. The argument is an old one, that health, wealth, or beauty are signs of God's favor, and misfortune is a sign of divine displeasure.

Job had to fight that one through. Most people get a taste of the struggle sometime in life. But, the gospel Jesus, in fact, shows a distinct preference for ordinary people, women and men alike. He seems to be drawn to the less blessed in health and fortune than the rich and high powered. He likes unpretentious sinners. He has harsh things to say about high faulutin' hypocrites.

Many times I have been struck with the majesty and power of Christ. Once, standing in the nave of the Monreale Cathedral in Palermo, Sicily, gazing at the mosaic of Christ-Creator in the apse, I knew what awe was. Art and music can make the spiritual accessible. Gregorian chant has always created a sense of the other world for me.

Meditating by candlelight before an Ethiopian icon of Jesus creates for me a realization of a more human Jesus. Could he have had a sense of humor? I could think of Jesus as having humor. I could even speculate about his moments of sadness or loneliness. But his full humanity was far less thinkable than his greatness, power, majesty and perfection, and his unworldly reality.

Two facts have to be squarely faced: first, Jesus was truly human. Second, nowhere in Scripture does it say that he was celibate.

Most Christians can recall moments in which the presence of Christ was palpable, indelibly memorable, when the humanity of Christ became true for them. Raised Catholic, I envied some of the songs my Protestant friends sang. "The Old Rugged Cross" somehow made the crucifixion more alive for me than most of the hymns that we sang in our church. One tune I surreptitiously sang to myself was "He walks with me and He talks with me and He tells me I am his own." I couldn't find any other song that gave me quite the same comfort of Jesus' accessibility—and his common humanity.

One pivotal experience shifted my fundamental understanding of Christ, of Christian teaching about sexuality and, the tradition of celibacy. The movement, for me, was a profound epiphany of the fact of Christ's Incarnation beyond experience, myths, and the images of Christ I had valued.

When my son was five years old, we were walking down the center aisle of our parish church that had been recently redecorated. He looked up at the new, near-life-sized crucifix hanging over the altar. He said, "Look, daddy, Jesus has a penis." And indeed, like the honesty of the child who saw that the emperor had no clothes, he opened my eyes. The hand-carved, imported corpus did have a loin-cloth to satisfy us more repressed parishioners but the anatomically correct figure was complete, clearly perceptible beneath it without undue imagination.

For the first time in my life I realized that, yes, Jesus must have had a penis. He was like us in every way except sin. And it is no sin to have a penis. But his nature was complete, which means that he had normal erections. No sin there. During his thirty-three years he would have had to experience spontaneous ejaculations, with all of its attendant feelings. Natural. No sin there. Just incarnation, like us in every way.

Some people proceed from these simple, undeniable facts to speculate that Jesus was married—using the logic that marriage is also natural. The oldest and most constant tradition in that regard is that Mary Magdalene was his lover-spouse. She was a principal player in the life of Christ. Feminist theologians have brought significant attention to the rightful place of women in Scripture.

But the Scripture does not give any clear and explicit evidence that Jesus was married or sexually active. And there is more substance to the idea that Magdalene was a lover than the more modern speculation that Jesus was homosexual in his orientation and loves.

Proponents of this theory give as proof the mutual love between Jesus and the apostle John and a biblical incident from the Gospel of Mark where one of the disciples ran naked from the scene of Gethsemane when a guard grabbed onto his robe.

The most predominant tradition is that Jesus was unmarried and celibate. But nowhere in Scripture does it say so—Scripture provides no clear and explicit evidence. Some Church historians claim the tradition of Christ's celibacy was firmly established and universal even for all the apostles after Pentecost.

That thesis is dubious if one takes Saint Paul's epistles seriously. Most scholars are not even interested in the debate. But none of the theories is more than that, theory. The celibate theory is sometimes the most defensive about the sexuality of Christ, depriving him of the most obvious and reasonable function of his sexual nature, the pleasure experienced with a spontaneous emission, as if pleasure were the sin. In embracing the theory of the celibacy of Christ no one should be drawn into the mistake of desexualizing him.

It seems to me brilliant and inspired that Scripture does not speak directly on the sex life of Jesus. Jesus is the person for all, not just some. The choice of celibacy to be like Christ is no nobler than the choice to be married to be like Christ. Jesus was the perfect moral model in truth and justice, love and service. Divinity was bound by nature—the limits of physical incarnation required one gender. This fact does not institute male superiority. Scripture leaves each of us free to speculate on Jesus' sexuality, but his moral perfection is clear and explicit. Truth and love are supreme in his example. They are imitable by any gender, in any sexual orientation and in any sexual commitment. Most folks seek their salvation, and their imitation of Christ, through married love. Some have consistently followed the path of celibacy.

Much of moral teaching on sexuality has been sidetracked by "act" orientation. Questions used to be common, such as "Is it a sin to French kiss? How far can I go without committing a mortal sin?" Such thinking distances us from the reality of life and is inimical to Christian life. Imitation of Jesus—as all life—is rooted in relationships—relationship with Christ and with him through others: "What you do to one of these, the least of my brothers or sisters you do to me." The act is measured in connection with the relationship.

And sex is fundamentally about relationships. I recall with perpetual bewilderment the comment of a brilliant moral theology professor who later became a bishop. He was asked by a bold and less brilliant theology student, "Why is masturbation a mortal sin?" The professor's response was underscored by his manner of delivery. He rose to his full height, expanded his chest, placed his hands on his hips beneath his black cincture, and said "If it were not a mortal sin who would get married?"

Most married people find that thinking abhorrent, demeaning, and ridiculous, as if simply any guilt free sexual pleasure could be a substitute and therefore a threat to the love, devotion, companionship, and all the concomitant blessings and strains of a committed, married relationship.

Celibacy is also a way of relating and a way of loving, living, and serving. Men and women who strive for celibacy are also gravely hampered by an attitude that conceptualizes it as simply sex-act-free rather than a fundamental relationship with self, others, the world, and the Divine. Celibacy is a distinct way of coming to terms with sexuality, just as marriage is. Each is grounded in distinct ways of relating.

Christ is the model for the married and the single, the celibate and the striving. Clericalism—that special and elevated privileged perch carved out for clergy—in fact does the Church and celibacy harm. It hijacks Christ and makes him like clergy, rather than all of us like him. Clerical celibacy shortchanges itself and handicaps those who wish to practice and achieve it in bypassing nature by spiritualizing it prematurely and beyond reason. A person who wishes to live celibately must be just as in touch with his or her sexual nature— and arguably more so—than one who plans to marry.

Christ does not love celibates more than the married, and the married do not love Jesus less than the celibate. Marriage and celibacy are each modes of using one's sexuality in honest, productive relationships where truth and justice are supreme—a space and time in which Love comes alive.

8

APOSTLES:
HUMAN LIKE US

*The celibate and the virgin have,
in truth, put on Christ*

CLEMENT

The appropriate title for this reflection should be "Men and Women Like Us." Celibacy is not the prerogative of men or clerics. Women for millennia have dedicated themselves to celibate service with scant notice and little credit. They have, however, been integral to the development of the practice and the excellence of the charism.

There are those who argue that celibacy was the universal practice of all the apostles, including Peter, after Pentecost. The point of these apologists is to establish an ironclad apostolic tradition for celibate legislation for the priesthood as we know it today. The history of clerical celibacy, including the testimony of Saint Paul, defies that point of view. My intent here is not to enter that debate but to reflect on the persons of the apostles and the followers of Jesus as he chose them. It is not reasonable to hold that Jesus attracted only disciples who were practicing celibacy when they began to follow him, nor did all the early Christian disciples eschew marriage. Not all of those who followed Saint Paul's wish for celibate living were "presbyters."

Scripture does not say anything directly about the sexual life or adjustment of the apostles either before or after Pentecost. We only know that Peter had a mother-in-law. That fact alone tells us nothing about his sexual adjustment. We cannot use exegesis to help us reflect on the sexual development of the apostles. But an alternative is to turn to an ancient tradition of eisegesis. That tradition is, as Webster says, to interpret a text of the Bible by reading into it one's own ideas.

First, I make the assumption that the followers of Jesus were folks just like you and me, average people for their time and place. Second, I assume that they had a more or less normal sexual life and development preceding their encounter with Christ, and that their transformed sexuality endured beyond their conversions. Third, the Jesus community lived the gospel story with associations and emotions not recorded by the evangelists. Granted they may have been average people; however, they were involved in a drama of gigantic proportions and epic consequences. Its repercussions have echoed through the centuries and encompassed us all.

I construct my meditation in a drama of three acts centered on scenes of the anointing, the passion, and the resurrection. The cast of characters is Jesus, Peter, Judas, John, and Mary Magdalene.

The impulsive Peter is a man who can fearlessly brandish his sword in the face of armed attack and yet a few hours later whither before the innocent questioning of a servant girl. Of all the apostles, he is the common man. Opinionated and vocal, he is burdened with the compulsion to "look good" and be accepted, which repeatedly leads him into embarrassing compromises. He always remains a bit of a crowd-pleaser. He was a married man, and there was a constant tradition in Rome up through the eighth century that he had a daughter.

What can we say of John, the idealist, and enthusiast? He perceives and presents himself as a lover. His manner disarms. He goes freely where others' timidity or belligerence blocks entrance. A ready smiler, a beguiler in whose visage every mother sees a son, every friend finds a confidant, every woman feels a reverent magnetism. Tradition portrays him as a young man, and a bachelor.

Judas has been villainized by centuries of symbolization for his role of confidant-turned-betrayer. Clearly, this characterization does not exhaust the richness of his personality. He was a bright man, perhaps the first to grasp the dimensions of the messianic vision. Ambitious and driving, he was a natural leader and the one of all the apostles most capable of practical decisive action.

He held the purse strings. His very presence inspired confidence. So trusted was he that his exit from the Passover table was neither comprehended nor questioned. Intensely devoted, he was equally jealous of his position, his talents, and his loves. He was the special leader among the group and, after Jesus, the one who inspired the deepest feelings of personal trust. Given his maturity, he would have been married according to Jewish custom.

Married or bachelor, at least prior to, and probably during, the early months of association with Jesus, these three men lived lives sexually indistinguishable from other men of Palestine.

Modern scholarship speculates that there are three separate women involved in the story of the anointing at Simon's house, the anointing at Bethany, and the woman at the foot of the cross and at the tomb. But older scholars, like F. Prat. S.J., allow for the possibility that the women are all one and the same. I have chosen to follow his interpretation because the beauty of the idea that a prostitute, from whom devils were cast out, could become the beloved and trusted friend of Jesus is too precious to disregard. This woman is the sign of hope for all of us. Her humanness renders her even more accessible than Christ's mother.

Magdalene, by constant tradition, was a prostitute prior to her association with Jesus. This does not mean that she was a cheap or uncultured woman. In fact, quite the opposite seems to be the case. She presents herself as a worldly wise, cultivated, and advantaged woman. She could afford expensive luxuries that she lavished on her dearest friend. Her actions exude an air of the dramatic mixed with modesty and finesse without crudeness.

This is neither an anomaly nor is it astounding when we recall that Eastern culture elevated the role of prostitution to a religious and ritual level. The idea of prostitution at the time of Jesus should not surprise anyone. Saint Thomas Aquinas labeled prostitution "a necessary evil." Pagan temple prostitution existed throughout the Middle East, but these women (or men) would be anathema to any practicing Jew because that contact would carry the stigma of religious infidelity. But many prostitutes freed from any religious ties were held in a certain amount of esteem. Some were "courtesans" in the long social tradition that persists even today to some degree. The apostles would have access to the women, perhaps of a rather exalted character, because of their notoriety in the city.

This is part of the atmosphere in which our eisegetical meditation proceeds.

Act One: Luke sets the scene for the first act of our drama. He tells the story of the anointing at Simon's house simply. A woman, a sinner, came to Jesus at the table of a Pharisee's house. She brought a jar of precious perfume and stood behind him at his feet. She began to bathe his feet with her tears, dried them with her hair, kissed and anointed them with oil.

The invitation from the Pharisee to Jesus for supper would have extended to at least a few of his retinue; to do otherwise would have been improper.

Peter, John, and Judas are likely companions. Jesus reclines in the place of honor next to the host. This place is not one accessible to any casual passerby, but is located at the honored place at the front of the hall. Magdalene does not sneak in unobserved. She crosses the room, from entrance to the place of prominence, and stands behind Jesus at his feet.

Several around the table know the woman. Their silent signal to the host makes it clear that she is welcome as far as they are concerned. No one knows what she has in mind. This is no staged event. It is a dramatic encounter. Falling on her knees she cries with the passion of one who is shaken to her foundations, her sobs and tears, uncontrollable.

She uses them to perform the ritual washing of hospitality. She lets down her hair, an act of humiliation, to wipe the feet she has cleansed with her tears. She anoints Jesus' feet with the expensive oils she has brought with her. Emotion draws in everyone there. The host knows the woman too. Jesus does not. The host knows of this unfamiliarity and thinks with a sneer, "If this guy were a prophet, he would know that this gal is a prostitute." She has enough social acceptance to allow her entrance into the house and banquet uninvited. But why does she come and intrude into this particular dinner?

This is no chance meeting. Magdalene had prepared for it meticulously. Hers is not a spur-of-the-moment conversion. She is a public woman. A prominent woman, she has to declare her change of heart publicly in an unambiguous, even a dramatic, way. She is changed.

How has she come to be so profoundly moved by this man's teaching? She never met him. How is it that she is so confident about his reaction? Why does she presume on his kindness and power without any reserve, even with a kind of familiarity? Her status and station in town does not lend itself to mixing with the common rabble that crowd around Jesus in the streets and temple square. How has she come to know his manner, his custom, his movements? How did she know he was going to be here?

The scene is not the beginning of a conversion. It is the result of a profound metanoia. The encounter is a symbol and acknowledgment of the change that has already taken place.

Someone has been instructing her. Some people close to Jesus are close to her. Men who changed little by little before her eyes and possibly in her arms. Some men in whom she could see a transformation, who were living proof of the effectiveness of his teaching convinced her of Jesus' capacity to change lives, to forgive. She was confident he would be accessible if she too could get close to him.

What brings our principals together? Why not Magdalene's profession? Could not Peter and Judas who were separated from their wives and on the road seek the consolation of a prostitute? There is no tradition of male chastity in either Eastern culture or Hebrew tradition at the time of Christ. Certainly celibacy was alien if not abhorrent. Would they not want to instruct and mentor their young unmarried friend, John, in the normal process of growing up? Is it even possible to think of these men—no matter what their subsequent development under the grace and tutelage of Jesus' presence—as anything but normal, average people at the point when they met Christ? In the time of Christ, prostitutes were not stoned to death or ostracized. Adulterous men were not held in disdain. Only adulterous women bore the full wrath of the law. Why should we find it permissible, even edifying, to recall the prostitutes of Scripture, but consider it unthinkable or shocking to realize that the men of the Scriptures—saints—had sexual lives and developments like us?

Although Magdalene could see the changes in Peter and Judas, she was most intrigued by John. He may have been the principal instrument of her conversion. Judas may have introduced them, since he was the one who knew the stylish apartments and boudoirs of the city. And Peter's high spirits and impulsiveness may have led him also to Magdalene's house.

John's youth and inexperience made him interested and vulnerable. Judas and Peter, like good older brothers, and in keeping with custom, time, and place see to their friend's sexual initiation. It's common practice and expected.

Magdalene's conversion capped by Jesus' acceptance leads the apostles to a reconsideration of their own sexuality. Sex turned into friendship is transformed into love. At least it is the beginning of discipleship beyond sexuality—an invitation to celibacy.

The first act of our drama introduced our characters and established their interconnections. The second act of our drama portrays the growing tension and the internal conflicts of our players. Mary the Magdalene is identified as the woman "from whom seven devils were cast out." This is her self-portrayal. Life prior to her religious experience looks ridiculous, vacuous, and positively evil in comparison to the richness and meaning of her current life as one of the band of women who travel with Jesus and his disciples and minister to them.

Every act of the day, every chore, every encounter, every friendship is infused with a love unimaginable to sexual exchange alone. Her love has expanded beyond sexuality. She inhales it in association with Jesus.

Act Two; Scene One (several months later): Our principals are at a suburban home where Mary Magdalene is with her brother and sister. Some people want to see the Bethany Mary as an entirely different person. I like to see her here in a setting made possible by her new life, now normalized. Her brother and sister are drawn into the realm of Jesus' influence by her example. Thus, the circle of love grows naturally, organically.

Mary, the perfect hostess, washes and anoints Jesus' feet. The act is reminiscent of the earlier anointing, but now the contact is one of assurance, gratitude, and familiarity. The joy is not entirely without alloy. There is a foreboding related to the intensity of the Jesus-talk, both pro and con. This is a moment among friends, isolated from the opposition. It is a precious fleeting time, like the comfort of dusk.

Judas is in a different mood—petulant. He voices disapproval at the way Magdalene is lavishing expensive oils on Jesus. He wants to see the oils sold and the money given to the poor. Jesus rebukes him gently. In the end, John will call Judas a thief.

At this Bethany anointing, Judas shows his resentment toward the deepening relationship between Mary, John, and Jesus. He is not just questioning the use of her money. Judas dislikes Magdalene's place in the apostolic community. He may have enjoyed her favors, but no longer. He now thinks of her as a slut with high and mighty airs. She had been quality; he selected her after all. But he cannot abide the thought of her equality.

What distinguishes John and Peter from Judas is not their earlier sexual behavior, but Judas' inability, in the end, to apply the Jesus message to his daily life and associations. The master lives and teaches that love, mercy, peace, and forgiveness should be conferred indiscriminately. Judas cannot live as the master teaches. The vision of success and specialness feed his ambitions. Now he is disillusioned. His vision destroyed.

Act Two; Scene Two (night has fallen): The Passover supper has ended. Jesus and Judas come face to face in the garden of Gethsemane. They approach each other slowly, tentatively. The cautiousness is born out of singular emotion and severe strain on familiarity and friendship. The setting is not new, a comfortable garden retreat. They all have been here many times before. They know each other well; they have shared intense moments. Now the approach is strained, uneasy. Death is in the air.

Jesus' cheeks are tear-stained and his robes rumpled. Judas, whose confidence and casualness usually hangs easily around his shoulders, is uncharacteristically jumpy. His eyes and the slight change in his gait tell the story. Jesus asks the question, "Why have you come?" Judas says nothing. They exchange their usual greeting, an embrace, a kiss.

There are observers. A small group loosely follows each to the spot—to this moment. Jesus' friends are a bit tipsy—addlepated by celebration and sleep.

The other group is purposeful and professional. At first one misses the weapons. Neither group is fully aware of the decisiveness of the confrontation. Peter impulsively draws his knife and cuts a soldier's ear. Jesus restrains him.

Only two men are aware of the emotional strain and the intensity of the inner struggle that have brought them to this juncture. None knows the crisis each member of both groups will face in the next hours and days.

Act Three; Scene One: Jesus in agony hangs on a cross. His executioners are milling nonchalantly around the area. Mary Magdalene stands as close as possible. John her faithful friend supports Christ's mother. The tears of loss and suffering have no words. Peter cowers on the outskirts, pretending he is not involved. He presents himself only as a curious outsider. Judas, our other principal is out of sight; he hangs himself. Each is overwhelmed with unspeakable emotion. Each reacts according to character.

Act Three; Scene Two (early Sunday morning): Magdalene is at the tomb of Jesus. She is doubly distressed because the body of Jesus is missing. Distraught and blinded by tears she does not recognize the risen Jesus when he approaches her. When she does, she is deliriously happy. "Quit hanging on me. I'll be around." Jesus says. While Magdalene runs to tell the others, Peter and John run to the tomb.

Our drama ends here. Whatever else it is theologically, historically, or symbolically, it is a human drama. These are real people.
They are believable, and they move believably in and out of each
other's lives. Their interrelatedness is evident. There are no miracles
here. There is no artificiality about the way their lives fit together.
When we consider them at the denouement of several years of association, we should remember the point at which they stood before
their introduction into the community. They, like us, are people in
process.

Real people have emotions. In our characters we see intense feelings, raw emotions. Powerful men do not commit suicide, coura-
geous men do not cower, strong women do not wail in repentance
and grief unless they are deeply involved and moved to the depths of
their beings. Is it reasonable and logical to think that only the woman
Magdalene had had sensual emotions, sexual feelings, and experience?

Magdalene, even more than Christ's mother, is the woman of the
gospels. She is complete. Humanness transformed by love. The male
disciples of Christ are equally human, bound by space and time,
psychically and culturally. Just like us. Sexual development and experience had to be part of their personal history and growth. Whatever sexual adventures they had in youth were not undone by their
call. Their sexual instincts were not abrogated by their conversion.

Sexuality, everyone's, is bound by space and time. To say that the
Jesus message transcends nature is not to say that it negates nature,
renders it invalid, or obliterates experience. It merely goes beyond
nature. All of the principals in our drama were transformed by the
Jesus presence and the Jesus message.

Crucial to an understanding of celibacy is the assumption that
the apostles had a sexual development as ordinary and normal as
any of us, and they lived a normal sexual life. If they embraced celibacy it was not because they turned antisexual or asexual. They went
beyond sex. You can be sure that their transformation influenced
every aspect of their lives, including their sexual behavior. That is
what growth and grace does—transforms nature.

9

PAUL:
CELIBATE PROTOTYPE

About remaining celibate,
I have no directions from the Lord,
But I give my own opinion.

1 CORINTHIANS 7:25

Paul the Apostle is the sole autobiographical witness to celibacy in Scripture. The significance of his prototypical declarations, validated by his life, can hardly be exaggerated for an understanding of the essence of religious celibacy in the Christian tradition. What may or may not be inferred from the life of Christ about celibacy is explicit in the life of Paul.

Paul came to his celibate intention and the *awareness of his personal capacity* in the process of a profound religious conversion. His earlier life most likely involved a wife since an unmarried man could not have risen as high as he had in the Jewish community of his day. Was he widowed? Could his wife have left him after he abandoned Judaism? Or could he have divorced her? The simplest argument is that his wife died. He certainly knew what sex and marriage were all about.

At any rate, his dedication to celibacy was a *free choice*, imposed by no agency or power, either earthly or celestial. In that sense, it was "natural" for him. He recognized that he was just as entitled to a wife as were the other apostles. And although he did not require the discipline of celibacy from anyone else, he could, from *experience*, recommend it to others, even for brief periods, to facilitate prayer and reflection on spiritual realities. His determination to be a celibate, like Gandhi's, was not institutionally bound—or necessary for his status as an apostle—but, nonetheless, it is clear that he bound himself in a *vowlike* commitment.

The sequence of Paul's ministry and his celibacy is clear. His conversion was to Christ. It was intense and complete. His inclusion as an apostle followed later from his work. He was not commissioned as the other apostles were. He was not a priest in the sense of the word as we use it today. He was unique even among the apostles. Like you and me, he did not have face-to-face encounters with Jesus before his Ascension. The important thing is that his initial celibacy was not clerical, but simply Christian, his ministry was apostolic and received the full benefit of his celibate dedication.

Remember that Saint Francis of Assisi, as I said earlier, was never ordained a priest. Only at the end of his life, at the insistence of his followers, was he ordained a deacon. In a way, celibacy has been hijacked by a clerical tradition. Paul never conceptualized the practice of celibacy to be reserved for clergy. His recommendation is broader, addressed to the whole Christian community and, in fact, not directed specifically at clergy. Some people tend to restrict celibacy to priests and religious. By placing marriage and priesthood in opposition, rather than celibacy and marriage as contrasting modes of living the Christian life, we miss the richness of the Pauline wisdom. Celibacy equally is meant to be for Christians simply to be Christians.

Paul concluded that celibate existence allowed him great latitude to *serve others* for his *spiritual motives*—love, personal love, for Christ and neighbor "on account of the kingdom."

A realist, Paul had no illusions that life was static or easy—he could name the difficulties he endured. He preached, wrote, traveled, and suffered in his service to others. He proved the purity of his intent by *work*—he supported himself at the same time that he did not deny that others could be worthy of support for their similar service. There was an intentional ethical integration to the *dynamic* of his life.

Paul's complete dedication to his communities is indisputable and his affection and care clear in his epistles. His devotion was all-absorbing.

Celibacy was proven in Paul's *community* building—his loves, if you will. Those loves were all inclusive. The experience of universal love seems to be part of the integrated and achieved celibate of Eastern—Buddhist—as well as Western religious traditions. Paul expressed it as a *lived experience*. In the words of Paul's great love, Jesus Christ, there was no distinction between male and female, Jew or Greek, slave or free—all are one.

Repeatedly in his personal revelations, scattered throughout his letters to his beloved "churches," Paul revealed a *radical honesty* about himself. He could, and did, number his faults. He could desire to do "good" and fail to do it. He tells of his own inner conflicts. Paul also reprimanded unrepentant sexual sinners. Thus, through the centuries, his actions inadvertently justified sermons of fire and brimstone from less integrated and more self-serving spiritual leaders than he.

Paul has been credited with fostering male domination of women. But some modern scholars have debunked those accusations by showing that part of his texts were altered by later revisionists who used their own additions to keep in place traditions that they felt were imperiled by Paul's teaching of an essential "oneness" and equality—all peoples belonging to the royal priesthood.

Paul reveals that he suffered a "thorn in his flesh"—an angel of Satan—to tempt him lest he become "proud." Almost all Scripture commentaries conclude that the meaning of the thorn is "unknown." When, however, one scholar or another ventures a guess, the conclusion is inevitably some physical infirmity like epilepsy, malaria, stammering, or Carl Jung's favorite, psychosomatic blindness. All agree that the bothersome affliction was physical and humbling. Paul prayed repeatedly that the temptation be taken from him only to be reassured that divine grace was sufficient for him to overcome his "weakness."

Why would Paul have been free from occasional sexual temptations, even after years of celibate practice? Would not sexual temptations have been humbling to Paul? Understanding the thorn as
sexual is so logical if one considers the persistence of the sexual impulse and Paul's courage and honesty. We favor Paul's radical honesty in disclosing the "thorn" for whatever he meant it to be.

Malaria would be a trite complaint for a man of such stature.
Eye trouble would be an inconvenience. Stuttering, hardly imagin-
able in one who held Greeks spellbound. Paul's humbling weakness
was central to the man he claimed to be, a celibate for Christ. He
considered his thorn a temptation not an illness. He tells us he has to
fight this temptation repeatedly, and with the grace of God he con-
quered it. This is human, real, and powerfully natural and honest.

Paul was not antimarriage or antisex. He comments on the mutual sexual needs of married partners and does not want them to
deny pleasure to each other. He does not distinguish between the
sexual rights of the woman and the man. He acknowledges the power
and naturalness of the sexual drive and sexual needs, and he wants
people to be in loving sexual relationships rather than to "burn." Paul
offers realistic advice. Sex and the sexual needs of others do not disturb
happy celibates. They contend with their thorn of the flesh just as Paul
did by prayer, work, and dedication to the community and love.

His personal choice and his satisfaction in the way he was living
are explicit. So much so that he could recommend it to others. He
says, "Try it for a time," you may like it, too. Paul thinks that periods of dedicated celibacy are an aid to prayer. Christian culture has
lost a sense or taste for a period of celibate dedication. Buddhism
retains that custom. I believe that the lack of development of refined
and discrete sexual moral reasoning is responsible for this deficiency.
Similarly, that insufficiency is responsible for too much celibate failure and even corruption. If moral reasoning can only tolerate black
and white, development and growth become severely hampered and
even distorted. Moral retardation becomes inevitable because the
standard is unnatural and unrealistic. Rationalization replaces reason, denial obliterates reality, and responsibility hides behind ignorance and in the darkness.

Paul's teaching on sex and celibacy is that the Christian message is to be a livable and lived witness to meaning. He interprets the importance of the gospel message for all human relationships in their entirety and beyond sex. Paul acknowledges that human sexuality is not merely an activity, but a quality of existence related to our bodies being temples of the spirit and our persons members of a royal priesthood. Sex is not just something we do, but who we are.

Hypocrisy—intellectual and moral duplicity—necessarily follow from a disregard of the vital elements and functions that make us who we are. We are not disembodied spirits, figments, or shadows, but real people who need to act and be redeemed. Guilt, ignorance, and fear are unreliable allies in making moral decisions. Freedom is Paul's answer. And it is a good one. The children of God, who accept their sexuality in freedom with knowledge and gratitude and behave honestly and reasonably, without rationalization, denial, or avoidance, whether celibate or sexually active, are on the right moral path.

The context of Paul's teaching is important for an accurate understanding of his valuations. At first, he thought that Jesus was going to appear in the Parousia—the Second Coming—during his lifetime. In part, this expectation explains the urgency with which he recommends celibacy. The fact that he was wrong about the timing of the Second Coming takes nothing away from the authenticity and power of his lived example.

Paul's lived example is so vital to understanding the essence, process, and dynamic of celibacy that I have italicized those elements in the text. I consider them so important that I reiterate them in schematic form here. Anyone who hopes to live a celibate life will do well to use them for a checklist for himself or herself.

Paul formed a clear *celibate intention*. It was not something he stumbled upon accidentally or committed himself to out of necessity or compulsion. He chose freely, without fear or guilt, to live a celibate life. He wanted to be celibate in spite of what others chose to do. He did not deny his earlier life *experience*. He was thoughtful and had a clear *awareness of his personal capacity* to be celibate. He would not "burn," in his terms, if he embraced a celibate way of life. With knowledge and *free choice* he entered a *process*. He was confident enough to know that he wished to make celibacy a life dedication. He made a *vowlike commitment.*

Certainly, Paul did not practice celibacy for motives of profit or prestige. Love, personal love of Christ, was his primary *spiritual motive.* That had not been an easy or instantaneous development with Paul, though it was part of the *dynamic* of his life. He grew in love. That love and celibacy made it possible and easier for him to *serve others.* That love and service gave him the vision and reality that love is boundless and extends to all equally and without exception was his proof of the value of celibacy. His celibacy was validated in *community.*

The process that is recorded in Paul is the history of a *lived experience.* Its proof is not in some kind of plaster or unimitable perfection. Paul was a man. His life was not without blemish. He admits it. The process of his celibate achievement was marked with multiple trials and temptations. Repeated temptations that bothered him. His humanity was capped by a *radical honesty.* There was no self-deception or hypocrisy. Paul triumphed by prayer, work, and love. Those are the graces that transform nature: his and ours.

10

ORIGEN:
CELIBATE MARTYRDOM

He was a man of steel.
He spoke as he lived,
And he lived as he taught.

EUSEBIUS

E arly Christian celibate writers were not susceptible to edifying others by accounts of their own lives. At the same time, they could be staunch defenders of celibacy as a way of life, and others would be left to record their virtues. Origen, born less than a century and a half after the death of Christ, was among the most brilliant early Christian theologians. His father was martyred and only his mother's intervention (she hid all his clothes) kept the eighteen-year-old from running to beg for the same fate.

Although Paul and the earliest Christian writers used the metaphor of "dying with Christ" as a means of spiritual identification, it was left to Origen to indelibly stamp celibacy as an equivalent and substitute for physical martyrdom. More research needs to be done on any link between understanding the sufferings of Christ and the strong streak of sadomasochism that has persisted in the sexual and celibate history of Christianity.

In T. S. Eliot's *Murder in the Cathedral*, Saint Thomas á Becket speaks these lines four days before his martyrdom:

Beloved, we do not think of a martyr simply as a good Christian who has been killed because he is a Christian: for that would be solely to mourn. We do not think of him simply as a good Christian who has been elevated to the company of the Saints: for that would be simply to rejoice: and neither our mourning nor our rejoicing is as the world's is. A Christian martyrdom is no accident.

Saints are not made by accident. Still less is a Christian Martyrdom the effect of a man's will to become a saint, as happens when a man by willing and contriving may become a ruler of men. Ambition fortifies the will of man to become ruler over other men: it operates with deception, cajolery, and violence, it is the action of impurity upon impurity. Not so in heaven, a martyr, a saint, is always made by the design of God, for His love of men, to warn them and to lead them, to bring them back to his ways. A martyrdom is never the design of man; for the true martyr is he who has become the instrument of God, who has lost his will in the will of God, not lost it but found it, for he has found freedom in submission to God. The martyr no longer desires anything for himself, not even the glory of martyrdom...so in heaven the saints see themselves...in the light of the Godhead from which they draw their being.

This twentieth-century encomium to martyrdom captures the age-old reverence expressed by Origen for martyrdom. Toward the end of his life, Origen wrote a treatise on martyrdom that conformed to his lifelong dedication to his faith. His writing is a reflection of how he lived. This conceptualization of celibate martyrdom has persisted into modern times. Celibacy is a special way of serving God and being used as an instrument of service and grace to the people of God. Understandably, the meanings of martyrdom were transferred to celibacy and later to the priesthood.

Origen credited Christ with bringing virginity into the world, and he saw virginity, modesty, and chastity as the very models of perfection. Yet he freely used sexual imagery—kisses, mystical marriage—

to describe the interaction between the "soul" and the "Word of God." The knowledge Scripture bestowed was "the truer, closer, holier kiss, which is said to be given by the lover, the Word of God, to His beloved, the pure and perfect soul."

At the same time that he used an allegorical method to explain Scripture, he was also a literalist and took the admonition of Scripture to "cut off the offending member" to obviate any sexual temptation and to allay any suspicion against his integrity. Origen's testimony to the excellence of celibacy—virginity—took the extreme and corporeal form of self-castration. Interestingly, this custom persists in certain Asian groups of celibates who consider this the crowning of their commitment. I have known an occasional Catholic monk who has followed Origen' example, but approval of the custom was not accepted in Origen's time—even then it was considered fanatical—and is looked upon as "crazy" today.

Origen's theology had a deep and lasting influence on the monastic movement—where celibate practice is an essential element of the life. Origen's ideas left a deep impression on the early monks of Egypt, and the history of spirituality is marked by his thought on prayer. His basic thesis about prayer is that "what is impossible for human nature becomes possible by the grace of God."

He saw prayer not as a series of petitions for favors, but an entrance into union with the spirit of Jesus. Not just a theoretician, he offers practical advice on how to prepare oneself for prayer. First, one is to cleanse the heart from sin. He admits that this cleansing involves a struggle—war with oneself is a continuing battle to "free the spirit of disordered affections." Actually, he viewed it as a contest against all passions not simply sexual feelings. In this process the person entering prayer—following the exhortation of the Pater Noster—must be reconciled with his or her neighbors. Lastly, to pray one has to reject internal and external distractions.

Early hermits and the monastic movement became the primary repository of celibate theory and life, and propagated the tradition in the Catholic Church. Celibacy was always considered essential to the monastic way of life. In the early centuries of the Church, the practice of celibacy was not essential to the priesthood, but later the connection between clergy and celibacy developed into a secondary repository for the tradition. The relationship of celibacy to the priesthood has remained a hotly debated issue throughout the centuries. That debate has been renewed and intensified recently in the wake of the incidences of sexual abuse by Roman Catholic clergy. Church legislation and repeated pronouncements by popes that reiterate that a celibate promise is a necessary condition for ordination have not quelled the controversy. Questions continue to swirl around that regulation and its necessity for ministry.

Origen was brilliant. At eighteen he headed the Christian School at Alexandria. This was a first-rate institution that trained students for a scientific education. The curriculum was as challenging as any as can be found in a university today: logic, rhetoric, natural science, geometry, astronomy, ethics (philosophy of life), and theology.

It is difficult to exaggerate Origen's influence on the early Church. He wrote six thousand treatises—only eight hundred are extant— and kept seven stenographers and additional transcribers busy. He was the founder of biblical science with his attempt to produce the first critical text of the Old Testament. He was also the first scientific exegete of the Catholic Church. He produced annotations, homilies, and commentaries on almost every book of the Bible. His *First Principles* was the first Christian manual of dogmatic and systematic theology. His analysis is fundamental to an understanding of theology today. Origen states that Scripture and Tradition form the foundation of Christian doctrine. The rule of faith is contained in the teaching of the apostles, but they do not answer the questions about the origin of the human soul, angels, devils, and so on, that is the work of theology. Two elements coexist: positive and speculative theology, tradition and progress. Christian doctrine is neither sterile nor stagnant; it shows a development and follows "the natural laws of growth and life."

When Origen was in his early thirties, he was already famous in Rome and around the Mediterranean. The bishops of Palestine asked him to travel there and preach to them. Even then it was uncommon for bishops to sit and listen to the preaching of a layman. This preaching, however, brought him and the residing bishops under severe criticism. Fifteen years after the criticism for these incidents occurred, when Origen was forty-five years old, more controversy ensued. The bishop of Caesarea insisted on ordaining Origen in the hope of avoiding more trouble and any further controversy because of the fame and popularity of this layman whom he admired. Instead, a rival bishop, who, according to a contemporary historian, was jealous of Origen's renown and celebrity, excommunicated Origen and claimed that his ordination was invalid because of his self-castration. How like the current tensions in the Church between super-orthodox and more liberal factions.

As far as I know, Origen never aspired to ordination. Origen's celibacy was his primary asceticism, his writing was his dedication and service. This fundamental stance continued even after his ordination. There is no question that his vocation to celibacy and to the priesthood were two separate and distinct vocations.

Origen steeped himself in the Bible, and especially in the gospel of Saint John; he wrote a thirty-two volume commentary on that book. Here you can find the core of his mysticism and his ideas of the inner life. They proceeded from Scripture and were lived in the spirit of Saint John. Origen, by constant study and meditation, distinguished the three senses of Scripture: the historical, the mystical, and the moral. Knowledge of Scripture is vitalized as we live it, and it transforms our self-knowledge into the life of the spirit.

I agree with Origen that self-knowledge is the basis of any spiritual life. The failure of celibacy most times has its roots in this deficiency. Little progress has been made in this regard in seminary and religious training. In part, this faltering progress is due to a failure to recognize the distinct demands of celibate living. The need for the frequent examination of conscience and asceticism in general have made their way into clerical textbooks, but their personal integration often does not meet practical tests. Mortification must be an ongoing lifelong effort. Spiritual freedom is not quickly or easily won. Detachment from relatives, worldly ambition, and property are not simply elective spiritual niceties. Most early proponents of celibacy consider these detachments as essential conditions for celibate achievement. Daily attention to study, primarily of the Scripture, along with fasting are also necessary if one hopes to be celibate. Two millennia have done nothing to diminish the requirements for celibate service. Certain factors are unchangeable in this transformation from nature to grace.

The second half of Origen's life was spent in Caesarea where he opened a school with the same curriculum and standards as he had established in Alexandria thirty years earlier. He was safe in Palestine from the indignity of excommunication that he suffered in his former home. He was caught in Arabia during the Decian persecution in 244 A.D., but was denied the quick martyrdom he had idealized his whole life. The tortures he suffered in prison, in irons, and on the rack broke his health, not his spirit or his faith. He had been released from prison when he died in Tyre in 253 A.D., at the age of sixty-nine.

Origen established in his writing and his life that those of us who cannot share the sufferings of Christ through martyrdom can achieve the same result through celibacy. The martyr and the celibate share the same ideal, union with the mind and heart of Christ. Origen's convictions are deeply inculcated into the foundations of monastic tradition and religious life. These convictions still have the power to influence lives today. His praises have largely been unsung. Origen wouldn't care. He placed a lot of emphasis on the virtue of humility. The practice of celibacy has that effect.

11

ANTONY: RADICAL TRUTH

*My book, philosopher, is nature and thus
I can read God's language at will.*

SAINT ANTONY

Antony was a layman (as were the majority of early practitioners of celibacy) who lived to the age of one hundred and six years. Most of his life was spent in the Egyptian desert as a celibate hermit dedicated to prayer and asceticism. Antony was an astounding individual who merited an image of being the ideal Christian ascetic and a model for a life consecrated to God. Antony's reputation created an immense and widespread fascination and curiosity. One year after Antony's death in 357 A.D., Athanasius, a bishop, composed a *Life of Antony*.

The story of Antony's experience as told by Athanasius came to be considered a rule of life in the form of a narrative. This unique biography had a tremendous influence on celibate spirituality, especially in the fifth and sixth centuries. Augustine credited it with a profound effect on his own conversion.

Accounts of Antony's struggles against devils and demons under multifarious forms are legendary. They have been recorded time and again over the centuries in art and literature. Gustave Flaubert wrote *La Tentation de Saint Antoine* in 1856. He subtitled it *A Revelation of the Soul.* Hieronymus Bosch rendered the most notable visual depiction of Antony's spiritual tortures about 1530.

These struggles of Antony's against terrifying demons and gruesome hallucinations that tormented every one of his senses can be off-putting to some modern readers. But the descriptions of perceptual distortions described by Athanasius and others are consonant with the current understanding of the effects of sensory deprivation.

The history of celibacy clearly documents the development of human psychology. The progress of sexual/celibate understanding can be traced in the development of psychological awareness and the differentiation of inner stress and fantasy from externalized sources of conflict—"demons"—to inherent psychic ambivalence. As successive generations of celibates digested the experience of celibacy, the various elements of sexual striving tended to be recognized as internal forces. Feelings and ideas that were formerly attributed to forces outside a person are—as we say now—ego-alien. The "unthinkable thought," obsessions and compulsions, neurotic attachments, and even psychotic ideas and behaviors were attributed to the devil and evil forces. Epileptic fits were usually attributed to a visitation from the divine power. In the first five centuries after Christ, an awareness of the inner conflict of good and evil developed gradually; fewer and fewer phenomena were projected outwardly. It is difficult today to justify one's behavior by saying "the devil made me do it."

The challenge remains to determine individual freedom. What part of deviant behavior is the result of an illness? What part is a moral failure? Radical truth is the answer to personal responsibility.

Celibacy is a deliberate choice of ever-greater freedom toward control—rational determination of all behaviors and eventually thought. Some people think that fear and guilt foster "control." Not so. As I said before, fear and guilt are extremely poor allies in making rational decisions. The discipline of celibacy is meant to unify one's inner consciousness in an abiding awareness. This awareness of reality, the source of the celibate's traditional wisdom, is often referred to as the presence of God. Fear and guilt do not control anything. A free person controls self out of the unity of his or her being.

Freedom, mastery, and self-control are not easily won no matter what psychological framework is used to explain the experience. There is a gruesomeness to facing oneself at the very foundation of nature. There is an intrinsic isolation to the struggle. Neither can be eluded if the process is genuine. The dark night of the soul is a real and necessary experience for the celibate.

The failure of celibacy by many people can be traced to an unwillingness to confront internal demons at a sufficient level to make them real combatants or masters of their celibate fate. Too few people face their sexual nature with its full potential for positive and negative deeds. The celibate candidate must face the power of sexual instinct and the fullness of personal lusts as Saint Augustine defines lust. Those lusts are capable of the most profound self-deception, rationalization, and duplicity.

The teachings about celibacy have been soft peddled. Celibacy has been falsely touted as an accomplishment that anyone can obtain if only he or she has sufficient good intent and will. This really is not so. Celibacy is a special vocation, a special gift. Years ago young boys were told that they all had a "vocation" to be a priest. Every Catholic boy had the calling, and it was his to disregard. If he was strong, he would respond; the weak turned away. Celibacy was, by inference, accessible to every young man. That is a cruel myth that cheapens celibacy at the same time as it belittles sexuality and marriage.

Celibacy is not easy. It is disservice to pretend that it is. Those who are constitutionally unable to be honest with themselves will never be able to practice celibacy, and history has demonstrated that their number is legion. When celibacy is authentic, it is rightly admired precisely because it is an achievement of the highest order. When it is an unwilled burden, it is a torment and an obstacle to growth. But both of those conditions are possible only in a person capable of radical honesty. When celibacy is feigned, it is a betrayal and a hoax worthy of ridicule, and pretense is inevitable in one who lacks radical honesty necessary to pursue celibacy.

From the life of Antony, and confirmed in the biographies of others, we can identify the essence of the vocation to celibacy. The call to celibacy is the vocation "to be." It is distinct from any vocation "to do." Celibacy can be compatible with almost any work. Vocations like science, law, medicine, farming, social action, or whatever have all been given witness by celibate practitioners as well as by priests and religious.

The vocation to the priesthood, however, is a vocation to provide a special, important service. As the vocations of celibacy and priesthood have been commingled, each has lost a sharpness of achievement. In spite of the theological determination that a priest is "another Christ," his being cannot in actuality be separated from his doing. Religious celibacy in many ways has abandoned an appropriate and essential context, namely, the attendant conditions Antony found necessary to the practice: detachment from material things, constant asceticism of the senses (fasting and vigils), unending prayer and basic isolation, even if in the context of a community.

Bishops and priests do not live this way. They do, and must, use things, build and administer buildings, lead in the midst of political conflict, teach, and take their place in a world of professional demands just as married folks do.

The clerical vocation as it is practiced today stands more at loggerheads with celibacy than it does with marriage. Celibacy and marriage are incompatible; the demands of celibate commitment obviate the demands of one's sexuality that lead to marriage, partnership, and parenthood. Marriage and family responsibilities do demand an involvement with material things and a certain degree of natural comforts to keep a sensible balance.

Some priests, both diocesan and religious, do successfully incorporate celibacy with their religious practice. But a majority fails to one degree or another, some miserably. This failure is partly what the crisis of the Catholic Church is all about. Many lay and religious women live in a more circumscribed ascetic context and in greater charitable deprivation than many members of the clergy do.

Celibacy has proven adaptable beyond the Egyptian desert of Antony, but to pretend that priesthood is the reservoir of celibate practice today is a fiction. We have to look deeper for contemporary models—Dorothy Day and Mother Teresa come readily to mind.

And we have to analyze current celibate successes and failures more carefully.

Antony was the prototype of a monk, and the basic principles of the life he lived were translated from his desert isolation to community traditions. Also, he left a broader legacy that continues even today in a variety of spiritual movements beyond the monastic and the celibate traditions. First, he insisted that the serious seeker of spiritual reality demand of himself rigorous self-honesty. He was required to have an "elder" or spiritual guide. The guide was not merely the source of advice about the aspirant's progress or absolution from his faults, but the recipient of the full truth—manifestation of conscience—from the seeker. I have argued for years with my psychoanalytic colleagues that the basics of Freud's methodology have deeper roots in Christian tradition and the Jewish Kabbala than most modern practitioners are willing to admit. The long tradition of reflection and self-examination—even the council to keep a daily record of internal movements that Antony proposed to his disciples—has contributed to the natural impulse toward contemplation and self-discovery. The search for truth was rooted in an inwardness, that "human capacity and appetite for locating the sacred, the real, or the divine in the inward depth of all things." That search cannot be separated from the "reality" of the self.

Second, Antony required the celibate seeker to examine his own state of mind every morning and evening, even recording in writing the reactions of his mind and heart to the innermost movements of his life. The modern movement of "journaling" as a process of self-awareness is not as new as it might seem.

Athanasius' account of Antony's experience was not biography in the modern sense of the word, a personal history. But it did stand as a model of later hagiography. Its thrust was new, and it ushered in a new literary genre that focused on the "sayings" of wise men. The narrative was extracted from holy men's experiences and captured their wisdom from the anecdotes and stories they told.

Sometimes original sayings were put in the mouths of the desert fathers to add weight to their observations. The core of desert wisdom and the goal of the celibate ascetic experience were "radical honesty"—first and foremost about one's own person—no deception, no illusions. Honesty was the foundation for every encounter with every person.

Reality, not myth, was the coin of the realm. The new literature of this genre reflected a dedication to honesty and realism rather than idealization.

Sayings of these wise men pay frequent attention to the problems of sex and celibacy. The space allotted for a consideration of nature and sex exceeds that devoted to the subject of prayer. The desert fathers (who for the most part were not priests, but hermits, monks, and anchorites) provide frank and direct accounts of the struggles for purity, chastity, and celibacy.

The powerful and persistent draw of sexuality is acknowledged over and over by concrete examples of temptations in thought, desire, and deeds. Antony's life and accounts of other early celibates are replete with advice on how to counter the pull of sexual instinct. They recommend working, fasting, praying, and a rededication to the ascetic commune. Although the majority of examples are sexual temptations occasioned by encounters with women, there are also instances of sexual desires for other men and boys.

The struggles for chastity often resulted in partial or complete defeat, but also repentance. The accounts of desert celibacy do not cover up stumbling, reversals, and outright failures, nor do they pretend that celibacy is simply a superior state of life. The monks of the desert are fully aware of the dynamism between desire and control. They tell tales of monks who indulge in fornication and sexual intercourse leading to a pregnancy, even after years of ascetic practice and self-denial.

Some of the men who came to the desert life were previously married. Part of their struggle for celibacy involved their longings for their former wives. These men were naturally tempted sexually by the memory of their earlier experiences. These memories are part of the natural course of events for anyone seeking celibacy. Could anyone considering celibacy expect anything less? Other anchorites brought sons who were "scarcely weaned" to their new way of life. Some monks left their celibate practice and married, only to return to the desert to do penance for having left what they called the "angelic order." They considered their fall to marriage a "coming to impurity."

The body of Desert literature is unique in the history of celibacy. It is exciting and helpful precisely because it is so honest, real, open, and unvarnished. The personal histories reach out to us as those of fellow travelers whom we can understand, and, what is more, we can find self-understanding in them. The heights of spiritual achievement are unashamedly grounded in sexual nature. As Saint Bonaventure said, "The road to God always begins in the sexual appetite." Nature, in the way we are considering it here, is not the enemy of the spirit; nature is the road to grace and spirit.

One anecdote anticipates and foreshadows the predicament of modern public figures such as some bishops and cardinals who have compromised their celibacy. An anchorite, who gained great fame and was universally admired, sinned with a woman. But no one knew about it. Overwhelmed with guilt, he returned to his cell and locked himself in, refusing to see anyone. He did severe penance in isolation for a year. Even the brothers who came to him for spiritual advice were turned away; none knew why. When anyone came to his door, he simply asked for prayers. He did not know any other way to reply. He did not want to shock his listeners by telling them what happened because "he was of great repute amongst them and considered as a great monk." Certainly, part of his motivation was to save the Church and his way of life from creating scandal.

The dilemmas of celibate failure are not simple. Radical honesty does not require an unbounded public confession. But truth does demand self-confrontation and the protection of victims and the faithful. Confidentiality can be guarded in the service of truth. Secrecy will always be self-serving and destroys the very accountability and transparency Antony and the desert represents.

12

CASSIAN:
THE CELIBATE PROCESSS

He is found to be the same at night as in the day,
The same in bed as at prayer,
The same alone as in a crowd.
He sees nothing in himself
That would embarrass him if exposed to everyone.
Nothing that God sees should be concealed from human sight.

CASSIAN

J ohn Cassian is not a name that is currently bandied about in
spiritual circles. That is not for want of his importance. He
contributed more to the fiber of celibate understanding than
any other spiritual writer. Even Ignatius was touched by his spirit
during his retreat at the Benedictine Monastery of Montserrat after
his conversion and prior to his pilgrim life and the development of
his Exercises and the founding of the Society of Jesus.

John Cassian was formed in the desert tradition of radical honesty. He was able to translate that experience into a description of
the process of celibate development and achievement for all of Western monasticism and religious life in general. He employed the literary
genre of the desert tradition. He presented his ideas using the revered
hermits of Egyptian monasticism as speakers. Not that Cassian was
lacking in the personal experience of celibacy and monastic life.

He and a boyhood friend, Germanus, who was some years his elder, began their search for monastic life in Bethlehem around A.D. 380 when Cassian was eighteen years old. The association of the two friends lasted twenty-five years and took them on a journey of exploration through the famous monastic sites of Egypt and the religious capitals of Constantinople and Rome. In these places, he was involved for a time in Church politics.

John started his search for celibacy when he was relatively young, but he was forty-five years old before he was ordained a priest. His ordination took place around the same time that his friend Germanus died. At this juncture Cassian moved from Rome and settled in Marseilles to found a monastery. In fact, he founded two monasteries, one for women that included his sister and the other for men. He was critical of other monastic communities in France for their lack of basic discipline. Monks wore rings, had extensive wardrobes, neglected fasting, and indulged in sleep. Although he makes no extensive list of celibate transgressions, there can be no doubt sex was also commonly part of monastic laxness. Early Western monasteries were a far cry from the discipline, dedication, and spiritual awareness of the desert fathers.

The transition from hermit celibate existence to celibate communities was a logical evolution that moved monks (celibates) from isolation to ever greater social involvement. John Cassian was part of this early passage. But it should be remembered that celibate spirituality is grounded in aloneness, if not physical, at least psychic and spiritual solitude. The trail of Francis of Assisi is from hermitage to hermitage. His followers built large communities and buildings on the foundation of the fame and reforms he stood for. Contemplation, always a component of celibate life, consistently has remained the mental hermitage of the celibate even in an active life. Ignatius of Loyola characterized the mission of his followers as contemplation in action.

Cassian is best remembered for his writings—*Conferences* and *Institutes*—that deal with prayer, grace, ascetic discipline, and rules for communal living. But his understanding of the process of celibacy remains the most prominent and unique part of his legacy.

Cassian discerned and analyzed six stages that led from continence through chastity to purity of heart. The celibate process begins with the cessation of all deliberate sexual activity. The second and third steps are more interior and challenging. Here one must control any of his obsessive sexual thoughts and even occasional desires roused by a sight or memory. The fourth step unites the mental and physical resources. It involves a tolerance of inevitable physical arousal without any mental—memory or fantasy—participation. The fifth step of progress in the development of celibacy leads to complete inner calm in the face of any external sexual stimulation, wherein a person finds sex "no more inherently stimulating than brickmaking or other crafts." The sixth and highest degree of celibacy renders the man sexually serene in sleep as well as during the day.

Chaste integrity controls erotic fantasies even during sleep. "At this point, the body has been restored to its 'natural' condition of moderate intake of food and periodic nocturnal emissions caused by purely physiological necessity. Heart and mind are able to focus completely on contemplation, discernment, the Bible, the needs of others."

The significance of celibacy as a process has frequently been obscured and even lost in legalistic and idealistic formulations. Ignored are the dynamic nature of physical, psychological, and spiritual realities involved in the pursuit of celibate discipline. This loss of touch with the reality of sex and celibacy obscures an essential point— celibacy is a process. One cannot live by ideal and law alone. Neglecting the process has hindered the development of religious celibacy throughout the centuries. At times the practice of celibacy has been reduced to a charade. That state of affairs threatens the clerical system today.

No spiritual writer has ever been more forthright and realistic about discussing the nature and functions of male sexuality than Cassian. He does not skirt the reality of inevitable sexual excitement, erections, nocturnal emissions, and internal and external obstacles to celibacy. He, like other monastic commentators, was conscious of the dangers to celibacy that women, boys, and other monks—and one's own body—could pose to the aspiring celibate.

Cassian's realism and directness does not mean that the modern reader can easily distill the heady essence of Cassian's insights from the mash of fourth- and fifth-century conceptions of human biology and sexuality. Puzzling and tiresome are the elaborate mental gyrations and discussions of the meaning and morality of nocturnal emissions in a man pursuing celibacy. Most off-putting to the twenty-first-century observer are the antiwoman, antisex, and dietary presumptions that invade the work. Nonetheless, the rewards of searching through Cassian's treasure chest far outweigh the efforts.

Later ascetics, like Gandhi, were not free from similar biases but, by experience, came to observe the same connection between gluttony and lust made by Cassian. The Indian celibate said that if one could control his appetite for food, he could control all his bodily urges. Both men fasted and restricted their hours for sleep. Each, however, sought truth and integrity, not merely deprivation, by means of his celibate dedication. Cassian defined the goal of the celibate person as being a condition where he is constant and transparent: the same night and day, in bed or at prayer, alone or surrounded by a crowd. "The celibate sees nothing in himself in private that he would be embarrassed for others to see, nor wants anything detected by [the Eye of God] to be concealed from human sight." Spiritual motivation was crucial to the success of the celibate process as was prayer and grace.*

I did not discover Cassian before I undertook my study of celibacy. Just the opposite. Through interviewing scores of priests and hundreds of their sexual partners, I came to ask the same fundamental questions that Cassian had faced. My own definition of celibacy and determination of the process as I discovered it were unaided by Cassian's wisdom. But I am gratified to meet a convergent thinker who added confidence to my twentieth-century observations. I have no problem acknowledging that Cassian's formulation is wiser and more grace-filled than my observations, but we both trust in the same nature that is inevitable to the process.

---

* (The finest exposition of Cassian and his thought is *Cassian the Monk* by Columba Stewart, Oxford, 1999.)

And I repeat the theme of this book: the celibate quest is profoundly personal and only achieved by discovering the living process in oneself and in one's own nature, not in anyone else's book. Cassian is conscious and explicit, as I am, that nature can take one only so far. Grace must crown the effort.

If there are any beneficial consequences to the horrors of the sex abuse crisis that has been exposed in the Church worldwide, they will involve a better understanding of celibacy, a reform of the training for it, and a rediscovery of our true sexual nature.

In the past decade, I have had to review the records of hundreds of cases of sexual abuse of minors by Catholic clergy. This sad burden convinces me that being in touch with one's own sexual nature is indispensable for anyone who wants to be celibate. However celibacy is defined, it is a process after all. And as we examine our personal progress, we need to be aware of the signs of progress and alert to the red flags signaling danger and failure.

After reflecting on the celibate search inspired by hundreds of priests' lives, I formulate the celibate process in a tripartite interactive model, based on nature and informed by grace.**

1. The celibate process begins with developmental relationships and personality patterns, many of which precede any celibate intention, but will vitally influence one's sexual and celibate adjustment.
2. There is a process of internalization of the celibate ideal from intention to achievement.
3. There is a sequential process that involves a series of crises necessary for the refinement of celibate forces from awareness to integration.

The relationship cycle begins with the Primary Other, the mothering experience, and one's fundamental genetic endowment. This cycle lays down nature's groundwork for all familial and developmental

---

** (A more complete exposition of my thoughts on the process of celibacy can be found in *Celibacy in Crisis*, New York: Brunner-Routledge, 2003.)

relationships. Next, formative and educational experiences are built on and incorporated into the prior endowments. The relationship with the talents developed and the opportunities offered allow one to master skills and choose an avenue for service and love relationships.

The refinement of the life cycle leads quite naturally to an ever-expanding awareness of the universal interrelatedness of all life. Of course, the crowning stage of relatedness is with the Ultimate Other. We all have to make our peace with the universe.

This is the cycle of natural relatedness whether one is Christian, Buddhist, or Atheist. The grace of celibate love and service is parallel to the grace of married love and service. Neither is higher or lower, better or worse. The criterion is the authenticity and the fulfillment of potential that nature offers to grace.

If celibacy is chosen as a way of life, one begins an adventure of discovery—of oneself and reality with a capital "R." One can only begin with an image and intention. Both are subject to constant revision and refinement as the maturing process proceeds. No one remains celibate for the same reasons with which he or she began the enterprise. Celibacy is a love affair. The level of love in a relationship cannot remain static and endure.

But image and intention are only the primitive tools one has to begin the quest. As one refines his or her intention to be celibate, the awareness of one's capacity to actually be celibate grows. These two steps are commensurate with Cassian's first steps of ceasing all sexual activity and controlling one's sexual thoughts and fantasies. Thirdly, one becomes acutely aware of the process and the necessity to discipline one's memories and fantasies that may increase in intensity as a person adjusts to a new interaction with self and others. At the point when one's mind and body are synchronized to the task, one is prepared to really practice celibacy beyond mere intention. With sufficient practice one may be ready to make a commitment. Gandhi found that he had to practice for five years before he was prepared to make a vow of celibacy. If I read Ignatius correctly, he felt that thirteen years of practice under various conditions of isolation and contemplation, service, and study were necessary to make a real commitment and to set the stage for the final process of integration and achievement or consolidation. I think that Ignatius' schedule is reasonable. If that is not his thinking, I still think his time frame is valid.

Celibacy is not an instantaneous achievement. It takes time. We can measure the normal stages of celibate progress just as one can measure the stages of a child's progress from sitting, crawling, standing, walking, and beyond, or mastery in intellectual development.

The initial stage of awareness of the cost of celibacy is oftentimes marked by a kind of depression—a sense not only of what is to be gained by this way of life, but equally, what is to be lost. Without this stage and conflict, celibacy can never be realistic or possible. It is preferable that this stage is confronted early in the process of celibate living. My experience with priests who have a history of sexual abuse demonstrates that some men don't encounter this stage until they have been caught and treated for their violation. Others fly the flag of celibacy, but it never becomes their true colors.

After one has vowed celibacy and lived it for a time, a growing consciousness naturally emerges about just how different and distinct from others one has to be in order to be celibate. Correlative to one's mindfulness that he or she is living a life without sex, the growing knowledge comes that many other folks are living active sexual lives. That awareness is marked by hundreds of practical decisions that need to be made daily. The celibate must be willing to be dissimilar, unlike everybody else.

Most people who seek celibacy do so in association with other like-minded people. In Catholic ministry, religious life, or monasticism, the relationship is not merely communal, but one based on dependent and authoritarian structures. For periods of time these structures provide external supports and guards for one's celibacy. But there comes a juncture when the celibate control has to shift definitively toward internal forces. One seeks celibacy independently of any external expectations or controls. Celibate practice and identity consolidate.

The fourth stage of celibate progress is marked by the struggle between loneliness and aloneness. Loneliness is an inevitable condition of all life and love. But after years of celibate living the question becomes, "Is it worth it?"

Loneliness is marked by a sense of nothingness, nowhereness, and aloneness in a negative sense. A psychiatrist friend preaches that one of life's tasks is to transform that isolation into the ability to live fully by transforming that negativity into positive reality. Here nothingness becomes the freedom of "no thingness." The loss of direction of no whereness, becomes the solidity of "now here ness." And the desperation of aloneness metamorphizes into the triumph and comfort of "all one ness."

This way of conceptualizing a major adjustment to the loneliness of the celibate process is more than a cute linguistic game. To move beyond the threat of sexual compromise one must penetrate the edges of sadness and loneliness to center oneself in the boundless freedom of singleness, separateness and divine aloneness. From this center one can truly achieve the final stage of celibate integration.

The path of celibacy is difficult. If it is your carefully chosen path, it is the right way to love and service. Cassian implies that the challenges met in the process may be daunting, but are rewarding. That is my experience of the celibate life observed. Real pain does not come from living the process, but from the failure to engage in the struggle. The reality of celibacy is glorious, like a diamond. Its pretense becomes a charade and is not like coal, but ash.

13

AUGUSTINE:
CONVERSION
AND CONFESSION

I fled him down the nights
And down the days.
I fled him down the labyrinthine ways
Of my own mind.

FRANCIS THOMPSON

S aint Augustine loved women. He had a longtime companion whose eventual separation from him was like ripping his heart out. Yes, he also had at least one mistress during the separation from the mother of his son. He adored his son (Adeodatus)—his Gift from God. He loved being a father. Indeed he was a lover. And all the greatness of his accomplishments, his profound capacity for friendship, his deep spiritual insights, the breadth and acuteness of his synthetic mind, and his immense longing for God would not have been possible without his earthly and sexual loves.

A contemporary of John Cassian, Augustine of Hippo embraced the tradition of the desert about radical personal honesty. He was not converted to the ministry and only accepted priestly and Episcopal ordination under protest. His conversion was to celibacy. He saw it as his vocation and his means of salvation.

His intellectual pursuits were always christened with a search for truth. But when he accepted his eventual responsibilities to the Church institution—burdens that the Desert Fathers lacked—he extended his insistence on truth and integrity to the whole ecclesial community. He gave his testimony to the truth of doctrine from the inside, recording his own personal struggles from nature to grace.

When I read Augustine's commentaries on the Gospel of John, I am amazed how his brilliant mind melds grace and nature in his explanations of the miracles. For instance, reflecting on the multiplication of the loaves and fish he not only marvels at the wonder of Jesus' magnanimity and sensitivity by feeding the hungry, but goes on to marvel at the greater wonder of a wheat harvest that comes from such small grains.

Some fine Augustine scholars, including Margaret Miles of Harvard, have interpreted Augustine's descriptions of his sexual exploits and drive as adding up to a "sex addict." By his own admission he was sexually active from the time he was seventeen years old. And he was enthusiastic about it. We all know his prayer for delayed chastity.

I do not read him as an addict in the modern sense of that word. In many ways it would be encouraging to read his insistence on his obsession with sex in that way, because so many of us today do suffer from addictions. Understanding the dynamics of addictions and how to deal with them is an excellent guide to dealing with sexual impulses and cultivating a celibate lifestyle.

Indispensable means of dealing with addictions require a radical self-honesty and a solid spiritual program, reliance on a spiritual reality, a community of truth, daily rededication, and constant awareness. That is the finest and most effective program of celibate practice I know.

However one chooses to read Augustine's sexual struggles, he is realistic about the strength and insistence of the natural drive. He is not merely a saint for sexual sinners. To see him as such is to distort the real meaning of his life and teaching. He is a saint for lovers. I came to an active sexual life in marriage after as many years in celibacy as Augustine had spent in sexual indulgence. We were both converted, not from evil to good or from good to evil. Each was a shift toward personal integrity and truth. Each person has a vocation to love in a certain way. No one fulfills his or her vocation without integrating sexuality with his or her loves whether in celibacy or in active sexual lives.

Augustine left a testimony of his sexuality, his inner life, and celibacy remarkable for his time or any other. His writing contrasts starkly with the genre of the desert where the authors concealed themselves behind the identity and narratives of others. Augustine was not afraid of direct self-revelation. He spoke for and about himself. Honesty and humanity make his autobiography timeless good reading.

The "therapeutic" unfolding of the text—the reader participates in the author's ongoing process of uncovering the layers of an inner-self—make it classic and fascinating. The author makes no attempt to cover up or revise his past mistakes or imperfections in the light of later accomplishments and insights. Certainly, the facts are not related in the glib "tell all" true confessions mode revealed on modern television and in autobiographical fiction of 2004. But he does not reject his past as if it were not part of him. He places his life in the eternal context. Augustine confides his ongoing suffering, loneliness, and sexual temptations as to a friend.

Undoubtedly, the book of his testimony suffers from the stylistic limitations of its time. One example has always struck numerous readers and me. Augustine agonizes over the guilt he suffers from an incident in his youth—prior to his seventeenth year. He and a group of his friends raided a neighbor's orchard and stole some pears. The degree and the intensity of the remorse he expresses do not fit the crime. Many others, less burdened with a psychoanalytic perspective than me, speculate that young Augustine and his friends took sexual advantage—or even gang raped—one of the householder's servants. This interpretation fits the man. He demonstrated his sensitivity to his times and his contemporaries in using a metaphor rather than explicit narration that would have been unacceptable. The same devotion is expressed in his failure to reveal the name of his mistress.

Augustine's insight into his own sexuality represents a psychological quantum leap toward understanding human nature. He embraced his humanity and did not project his dark side onto demons, devils, and external forces. He accepted concupiscence—drives and desires—as humanity struggling against itself. His example showed that celibate striving could be integrated with customary psychosexual development. Celibate lifestyle no longer had to cordon itself off in isolated desert caves deprived of human contact and solely devoted to fasting, sleeplessness, unending prayer, and menial busywork like weaving mats. He gathered a celibate community around him to protect celibacy, but also to provide pastoral care. His community opened broad intellectual vistas for exploration by dedicated celibates.

Augustine's self-accusation, "I was a slave of lust," stands as a reality to be reckoned with. Addicted or not in the pathological sense, most modern observers judge Augustine's psychosexual development to be "normal." He began an active sexual life in his mid-teens; fell in love with a woman with whom he lived for thirteen years, and fathered a son by her. That relationship was broken off to conform to the social convention of entering a "suitable marriage." He described the breakup of that relationship as a rupture of his heart—"a deep cut leaving a trail of blood." In the wake of that separation he took a mistress, without love, for about a year. His prayer, "Lord, make me chaste, but not just yet," has become proverbial. I can find no evidence that Augustine failed to love his longtime sexual partner.

Losses beyond the separation from his life's companion also wounded Augustine deeply. The deaths of his mother and his son followed closely on the heels of that emotional wound. Bereft of the loves forged or sustained by sexuality, Augustine was converted to celibacy. No doubt doctrinal elements were involved in his change of allegiance from his Manichean views to those of his mother's orthodoxy, but the affective conversion was from sexual expression to a celibate way of loving.

Spiritual conversion precipitated by the death or loss of a loved one is a common phenomenon. The wound of a profound love loss is one way to "hit an emotional bottom." In one way or another, nature—life itself—goads every person to come to grips with the meaning of existence through limitations and losses. The ultimate choice is to embrace life more fully or to die. There are multiple ways to live just as there are various ways to dance with death. Sex is not restricted to one path.

Conversion is not a one-time event. Conversion—and certainly celibate conversion—is an ongoing process of incorporating past experiences with the reality of one's existence. Celibacy was an integral piece of Augustine's conversion. Celibacy is not predicated on the absence of sexuality, the death of the sexual drive, or on a dearth of prior sexual experiences. It is a new way of loving and the ever-new unfolding of nature to divine grace.

Confession for Augustine was the lived witness—the actual practice—of celibacy. Augustine had a unique capacity for friendship. This talent for love enabled him to gather a group of like-minded men around him to support one another in their service to the community and their celibate striving. He also maintained contact with some of his youthful friends, like Alypius, who eventually became bishop of Augustine's hometown. By the way, Alypius had experienced sex with a woman, but was never intrigued by it, unlike Augustine who carried with him—as most folks do who strive for celibacy—the memories of love and carnal affection through a large part of their lives. The sexual drive is a near inexhaustible fountain. Augustine knew it and lived accordingly.

In extrapolating the essential elements of celibacy from all its early exponents, one must sift through accidental conditions and put statements in the cultural context of their thought, expression, and practice.

Without doubt, Augustine's ideas of human sexuality were distorted by limitations of the biological and psychosexual knowledge of his time. Male sperm was thought to be the "breath of life" conferred on the egg. Menstrual blood was "defiling." Women were sexually "incomplete" men. Woman was necessarily secondary to man having been created from his rib. Sexual pleasure itself is the essence of evil. Liquid intake and spices had a direct effect on sexual excitation. Loss of sexual fluid causes weakness, and so on. Augustine did not invent any of these ideas that today we call false or myths. It is no aspersion on him that he could not free himself completely from all the myths of his time.

In our age of scientific sophistication, gender consciousness, and sexual explicitness, Paul and Augustine take an unfair beating. They have been mischaracterized as unrepentant misogynists and unalloyed champions of patriarchy. That is simply not true. One thing is clear: Augustine could not have reached his status as the scholar and saint he was without the experience of sexual love and fatherhood he enjoyed. (We cannot justify the thought either of a preconversion Paul as an unhappily married man.) Augustine devoted time to counseling married couples and clearly states in his *City of God* that marriage should be marked by "perfect mutual companionship." He insisted in the *Confessions*, if only near the end, that men and women are entirely equal in mind and soul.

Augustine, like Paul, tackled a perennial mystery: what is the origin of evil? That is a most complicated challenge to the best of philosophers. It engages exploration from the cellular to the cosmic levels. Modes of discussing sin and virtue remain daunting to the most ingenious thinkers. Convergent thinkers have not yet solved the puzzle.

It is easy but ultimately unchallenging to supply absolutistic pronouncements about evil and good. Many people read the words of Augustine and Paul in those terms. But these men were more normal, more complex. Paul confesses that he doesn't always do what he wants. He knows what is right, but fails to do what is better. Augustine was not a one-dimensional man or thinker. His struggle for a Christian life was multidimensional, not just sexual. All concupiscence merited his intellectual and personal attention. He struggled with the ideas and realities of evil, free will, original sin, and predestination at a depth no other first-millennium author ever did.

The practical problems of good and evil constantly prevail in Augustine's writings and his life. Why do good people do bad things, and bad people become the agents of good? Somehow nature and grace are inextricably intertwined in life.

Augustine is a universal spiritual model, in some ways more accessible even than Jesus, because he is so much like us. We can measure the distance between his nature and the work of grace. We, like him, are searching lovers, truth-seekers, spiritual-strivers, mistake-makers, regretters, repenters, in short, men and women with restless hearts looking for rest in eternal love.

14

MERTON:
PRAYER AND PERSEVERANCE

What a fool I have been,
In the literal and biblical sense of the word:
Thoughtless, impulsive, lazy, self-interested,
Yet alien to myself, untrue to myself,
Following the most stupid fantasies,
Guided by the most idiotic emotions and needs.

THOMAS MERTON

Thomas Merton converted to Catholicism and entered one of the Church's strictest monastic orders—the Trappists—in 1942. His autobiography *The Seven Storey Mountain*, a book that recorded his life and especially his mental and spiritual processes skyrocketed him and his monastery—Gethsemani, located in Kentucky—into international prominence. Later, however, as he developed spiritual depth over his twenty-seven years in the monastery, he repudiated this bestseller as immature pap.

Nonetheless, I, like so many other young people in the 1950s, found Merton's spiritual childhood encouraging and inspiring. It gave us the sense of spiritual possibility. His *Seeds of Contemplation* that followed the autobiography influenced cadres of Christians to make a connection between meditation and meaning in their lives.

His subsequent writings have entered into the modern canon of spiritual classics. The seven volumes of his published journals reveal his humanity, inner struggles, and spiritual growth more directly and accessibly than any other Christian celibate writer since Augustine.

Many people feel personally close to Merton. This closeness is a tribute to the force and intimate capacity of his personality that shines through his writing. Merton communicated himself beyond his thoughts and words. I continue to read him. I have been involved from time to time in a Merton Study Group and ponder many of his early writings and profit from following his inner development re-corded in the seven volumes of his journals. I feel closer to Merton than I have any right to. Though Merton was always accessible, I never met him nor corresponded with him, as many others had.

In 1949, I worked briefly at Hospitality House in Chicago founded by Catherine de Houeck and listened as she spoke engagingly about her Trappist friend. Twelve years later, after I was ordained, I gave some lectures at Madonna House, her foundation in Combermere, Ontario. From reading Merton and meeting Catherine, I knew that she remained close to him.

Catherine's tone was that of a mother toward a restless child. Merton never forgot her involvement in his conversion and voca-tion. He continued to share his doubts about his vocation with her. Catherine told me that she had to remind him many times of the importance of his monastic life. Multitudes counted on his words and example. Merton lived on the cusp between the anonymity of a hermit and social stardom. He never quite resolved that intersection between a contemplative within walls and an activist in the thick of things.

My other personal connection to Merton was through the Men-tal Health Institute in Collegeville where psychiatrists and clergy-men gathered during week-long summer sessions to discuss religion and psychological concerns. I recorded the sessions during its first years and became the executive in the late 1960s. The Institute be-gan in 1953 and by 1955 the Trappists sent a group of monks to participate. In the summer of 1956 Merton was in the group.

His attendance was orchestrated by some of his New York friends so he could consult with Catholic psychoanalyst Gregory Zilboorg who lectured annually at the Institute. Merton was attracted to the thought of being analyzed. He corresponded frequently with his New York friends, some of whom had been in treatment with the famous analyst—an analyst to the famous. They were a match for each other. Zilboorg was neither kind nor gentle with Merton. He judged Merton to be attention grabbing and self-centered; certainly a case of the pot calling the kettle black.

Zilboorg maintained that Merton wanted to be a hermit in Times Square. Merton's humility in accepting the judgment is a tribute to his stature, and allowed him to use the consult productively.

From his monastic cell Merton did a dance on the cusp of his times. Psychoanalysis, self-actualization, civil rights, Vietnam War protests, yoga, Buddhism, and Eastern spirituality all gained notoriety and popularity during the half century during and after Merton's life. It all interested him. But Merton was no faddist. He had a solid core. He was in touch with—even ahead of—the spirit of his times.

Merton's warts, his repeated struggles with himself about solitude and celibacy, his need to focus his energies and interests, his conflicts with authority and community, only make him more accessible and even admirable to me. This is no plaster saint. Merton is real. The more exposure one has to the substance of Merton's life—assets, accomplishments, failures, and limitations—yes, even his faults, endear him to a follower. His choice of the cloister was a choice for celibacy. He did not enter the monastery to be a priest. His abbot chose the young monk's path to the priesthood. He also dictated that Merton should write. Both obediences Merton embraced with enthusiasm. Merton offered up all his talents to the cloister, for solitude in pursuit of celibacy. To abandon solitude, conflicted as this decision always remained, would have been to reject celibacy. Merton could not do it.

Young Merton, prior to his religious conversion, fathered an out-of-wedlock child but, unlike Augustine, he did not have the experience of a long-term love relationship with the mother or benefit from the joys of fatherhood.

The strict discipline and twenty-five-year confinement in the monastery, however, did not prevent Merton from falling in love with a young nurse, "M.," as he refers to her in his journals. He met her honestly while he was hospitalized for back surgery. It is no exaggeration to say that he fell head over heels in love with her. He manipulated monastic rules, his friends, physicians, and the system in general, conniving to rendezvous with her at various sites including a doctor's office, restaurants, and his hermitage. During the same period, he contacted her on the telephone and they exchanged love letters. He was conscious while receiving Communion at the community Mass that he was "a priest who has a woman" in spite of the fact that their "lovemaking," at that point, had stopped short of intercourse.

The picture Merton paints of M. is of a levelheaded, down-to-earth young woman. She was not impressed with his fame or his clerical status. She liked the man, not an image. Her genuineness, unencumbered with spiritual superficialities, taught Merton things about life, love, and relationships that he had never learned before.

The intimate moments they shared are preserved in Merton's letters to her—he burned hers when the affair ended—and his journal entries. His journals record the excitement and conflicts surrounding clandestine calls, meetings, and letters. The memory of the love affair—a picnic they celebrated on the grounds of the monastery one Kentucky Derby day was central to the experience—had a profound and lasting effect on Merton's psychological and spiritual attitude.

His illicit—from the vantage of monastic discipline—phone calls were reported to the abbot who threatened to take Merton's hermitage away from him if he did not put an end to the relationship. This pressure was a major factor in the termination of the friendship. The breakup was not accomplished without sadness and soul searching by both parties.

Merton had many moments during his celibate striving when he had considered leaving the monastery. He and his friend had several serious discussions about the possibilities of marriage and a future together.

This monk's affair is best understood within the total context of his celibate striving, personality development, and spiritual growth. Few priests have ever exposed the broad range of their humanity in their celibate striving as did Merton. But even he does not record his struggles with masturbation and other internal sexual stresses. But Merton did not want his noncelibate emotional escapade to be hidden. He wanted to be "completely open, both about my mistakes and about my effort to make sense out of my life."

Merton explored his love while never abandoning his life of prayer, duties, or intellectual pursuits. He was successful in incorporating his experience into the richness of his spiritual struggle for integrity and love. The love Merton experienced with this young woman led him to a renewal of his celibate commitment and rededication to his life as a monk. This, of course, does not eliminate the fact that the experience demonstrates a period of "splitting" his behavior from the reality of his moral convictions and social reality.

Merton did not try to justify his affective and celibate lapse. He could with sincerity write: "What a fool I have been, in the literal and biblical sense of the word: thoughtless, impulsive, lazy, self-interested, yet alien to myself, untrue to myself, following the most stupid fantasies, guided by the most idiotic emotions and needs." These are not the words of a man trying to rationalize or deny events that were mistakes.

Merton's retreat from the world was not a rejection of life or a repudiation of the world. His was an uneasy solitude. He was caught between the thrust of creativity and the desire for isolation. On the one hand, he resonated with the ideal of Saint Peter Damian that "whoever dwells in his cell for life makes of his whole body one tongue to proclaim the praise of stability." On the other hand, he struggled like Antony with the illusions of solitary life: "Not with objectified exterior devils but with the devils which are illusions about the self."

Each person's solitude—the inevitable aloneness of the celibate choice—entails the struggle with internal devils. There is no way to avoid the conflict. It comes with the territory, whether it be in a hermitage, a city parish, an office, or kitchen. The conflict is found wherever the person is.

While Merton was in the throes of his conflict over his involvement with M., he wrote, "the only solitude is the solitude of the frail, mortal, limited, distressed, rebellious human person, made of his loves and fears, facing his own true present."

Celibacy is in the now. The real, concrete struggle for celibacy is not in the mind trying to extol and justify ideals or in the heart trying to rationalize compromises. Mature celibacy remains a dynamic and sustained struggle requiring prayer and perseverance.

Just the year before he died, Merton presented himself in prayer as a "child, full of trouble, conflict, error, confusion and prone to sin." He pleaded that his whole life needed to change and admitted that he did not have the power to change. This is not the prayer of a novice celibate. This is the prayer of a man, seasoned in celibacy, immersed in a praying community. Above all, he is a man of truth, incorporating fully the radical truth of the desert. He did not cover up his failing, but he never ceased to try striving for completeness and integration.

Merton knew and lived Augustine's conversion to celibacy—an ongoing and ever-struggling life quest. Merton knew Paul's thorn in the flesh that would not leave him in spite of repeated prayer and sacrifice. He also lived with Paul's knowledge that the intention to choose the better and the higher did not always result in commensurate action.

The radical honesty and ongoing conversion of the committed celibate is united in its integration with all his or her human endowments—and limitations. Celibacy is not an abstract ideal. It is the achievement of an individual personality. Serious seekers of religious celibacy maintain that its practice and achievement are possible only if sustained by perseverance and prayer.

Merton's talent for putting spiritual ideas and ideals into words make his prayers and spiritual advice available to all of us. His honest struggles and especially his celibate perseverance in the face of his conflicts will remain a shining example for the ages.

15

NOUWEN:
CELIBATE LONELINESS

There is a deep hole in your being, like an abyss.
You will never succeed in filling that hole,
Because your needs are inexhaustible.

HENRI J. M. NOUWEN

enri J. M. Nouwen has become one of the most popular spiritual writers—with priests, religious, and laypersons—of the last decades of the twentieth century. His stature and readership have increased steadily since his death in 1996.

Among his forty books are journals, but not an autobiography as such. The body of his work, however, as a whole, as well as each individual book on its own, is personal and self-revelatory. All record his spiritual development and progress. He penned them in the form of essays for others. The intimate quality of his prose, free from self-absorption, renders his thinking accessible, classic, and profoundly appealing to a wide audience. He was the "wounded healer," "reaching out" as a companion to others on the lonely "journey to freedom" and peace.

I met Henri Nouwen in 1964 at the Menninger Foundation in Topeka, Kansas. We were both involved in training programs that focused on psychiatry and religion. He had already received his doctorate in psychology from the University of Nijmegen and would return there later to get a master's degree in theology. Brilliant and well educated, Nouwen became a professor at major universities, but in spite of his years in academia he was no academic in the essential sense. He was always primarily a pastor and, above all, spiritual. It was on that lonely spiritual plane that Nouwen fought his good fight.

My first impressions of Nouwen, tested over the years, have proved durable. Besides brilliant, he was gracious, energetic, inquisitive, kind without boundaries, generous, involved in all things human, and, at the same time, restless. He was like Merton in many ways. They were soul mates; Merton was the focus of Nouwen's second published book. Originally written in Dutch, it was issued in English as *Pray to Live* in 1970. But the geography that Merton explored mentally from the cloister Nouwen investigated on foot. He marched in Selma with Martin Luther King, Jr.; lived liberation theology in Central America, joined scholars in retreat, lectured in auditoriums and universities where Merton was only read.

Whereas Merton was a convert to Catholicism and a priest not by primary choice, Nouwen was Catholic to his core. He was typical of many vocations of men born to the faith. Priesthood was held in the highest esteem in every corner of his environment—home, family, community, school, and even country. To be a priest was his only goal. Typical of many boys from his background and era, he played at saying Mass when he was a youngster.

After our student days together, I maintained contact with Nouwen over the decades. He did a number of favors for me. A telephone call or a note was enough to merit prompt compliance. We got together when he was teaching at Yale and I at St. Mary's Seminary. Our paths occasionally crossed, at St. John's Abbey, Baltimore, and Washington, DC.

In 1986, Nouwen moved to Toronto, Canada, to become a chaplain to the L'Arche Daybreak community. L'Arche is a series of communities that care for people who are mentally and developmentally challenged, and where the disabled "heal" their caretakers. Jean Vanier and Pere Thomas founded these foundations of spiritual equality in France. The movement spread to Canada and the United States.

In 1992 I made a week-long retreat with Henri Nouwen at Daybreak. It was a profound experience for me. We celebrated Mass together each morning and prayed evening prayers with his small-home community. But there was nothing of the Ignatian silence or a respite from daily reality during that time. Quite the contrary, we were active, steeped in Scripture, as well as evangelization. I accompanied Nouwen as he taught an evening class—it was the account of the prodigal son—to the local L'Arche community. We went together when he met for reflection with an ecumenical group of ministers; I was in the audience as he lectured to several hundred people in a Toronto auditorium.

He insisted that I experience the L'Arche community. I ate an evening meal with one of the houses; aided feeding where necessary, and made rounds of the compound's workshops as Nouwen visited his brothers and sisters. Everyone is equal at L'Arche.

Although I already knew a great deal about Nouwen's life, what he shared as we walked and drove together from one of his commitments to another showed me an interior depth I had not suspected before, even from his writings. For all the seeking and restlessness of his basic personality here was the mature, seasoned, at home, settled celibate pastor.

I experienced Nouwen as a man of integrity. He said who he was—a priest—and what he was going to do—be celibate. He was who he said he was, and did what he said he was going to do.

For years I had been aware of Nouwen's successes. His books were bestsellers. He was well respected and sought after in the best universities. He was in demand for lectures across the country. He had a host of admirers. He was popular. As with me, he was a friend to countless people. Many people treasured him as a friend. But during this retreat I encountered for the first time in him the profound loneliness that is characteristic of a person who achieves celibacy.

Nouwen had wanted to be a priest from the time he was six years old. He was particularly successful in setting his own direction in his career. After the Menninger Foundation, he began a series of teaching assignments at Notre Dame, Utrecht, Yale, and Harvard divinity schools. His lectures inevitably led to a refinement of his thinking that resulted in the publication of the most current integration of his spiritual/emotional *Weltanschauung*.

Throughout his life, Nouwen retained the accent of his birth and education in the Netherlands, in spite of the fact that Nouwen's professional career as a priest was spent primarily in the United States and finally in Canada. Trained in psychology as well as theology, Nouwen blended his expertise into models of pastoral care filtered through his unique experiences and profound, psychologically sensitive spirituality.

In spite of his success and security as a university professor, Nouwen remained spiritually restless in the deepest recesses of his being. He interspersed his academic tenures with worldwide lecture engagements and extended excursions—to a Trappist monastery, an ecumenical research center, Latin America, and France.

At age fifty-four, he could say with the kind of humility, tinged with sadness, and radical truth that celibacy fosters: "I am still struggling with the same problems I had on the day of my ordination twenty-nine years ago. Notwithstanding my many prayers, my periods of retreat, and the advice from many friends, counselors, and confessors, very little, if anything, has changed with regard to my search for inner unity and peace. I am still the restless, nervous, intense, distracted, and impulse-driven person I was when I set out on this spiritual Journey." (*The Road to Daybreak*, New York: Doubleday, 1988, p. 127.) *Daybreak* changed that. Henri changed.

Nouwen, now my confessor and retreat master, encouraged me to reflect on death. I was sixty years old after all. My career, too, was winding down, my health uncertain. I continue to follow his counsel daily. Good advice: *Memento mori; memento vivere*. Remember death; remember to live.

Nouwen also had questions for me. He knew my book *A Secret World: Sexuality and the Search for Celibacy*, published the year before. He was also aware that I had lectured on human sexual development at two universities. We had spoken about homosexuality in the seminary when he came to Baltimore to lecture where I was teaching.

The questions now were personal; the subject was not academic.

In his final transition from academia at Harvard, Henri had been forced to struggle with his own sexual identity and orientation.

He knew he found his "home" and true vocation in Canada as a chaplain with L'Arche—this community of handicapped people and their assistants whose attributes and goals stood in such stark contrast with the lives of bright and privileged university professors and students. Here Nouwen was free to confront his own limitations— himself—in ways and on levels that were inaccessible to him in his roles as professor, author, psychologist, or preacher.

It was precisely at this juncture—when his restless search could settle its spiritual roots in geography—that he was to undergo a spiritual "dark night of the soul," and in psychic terms, a "break."

Nouwen was set up for the crisis. What might have brought satisfaction and been the final treasured goal of a seasoned professor— to teach at Harvard—occasioned a sense of failure and emptiness in him. He had suffered a deep disappointment at Harvard. And he sensed that they were disappointed with him. One who had always been sought after experienced the pain of rejection.

In the security of the unqualified acceptance and loving atmosphere of his new community, Nouwen opened himself up to a particular friendship as never before in his life. The conflicts found in this friendship, the possibilities of love were almost too much to bear. His integrity was stretched to the breaking point. If Henri had not been a man of integrity, the threat to who he said he was, and a compromise with what he said he would do, would not have caused the disintegration it did.

Even while we were in Topeka we had talked about the theory of "Positive Disintegration." That is the idea that in order to move from one level of personality or spiritual integration to another, a person has to relinquish the security of a stable state, go through a period that is experienced as disintegration, to achieve a higher degree of integration. Both of us had coached others in psychotherapy and spiritual direction through the process. The personal experience of such a break with one's past adjustment is distinct from and incomparable to the process of helping another person through it.

Nouwen, as was the custom of his whole life, kept a journal of his break. He wanted to know what I thought about publishing it. There was no question in my mind that it would be a gift just as his other books had been. The secret journal was finally published with the title *The Inner Voice of Love: A Journey Through Anguish to Freedom* (New York: Doubleday, 1990). He described the pain of the experience as a gift of immense joy and peace that revealed a new part of himself, "as if a door of my interior life had been opened [one that had been] locked during my youth and for most of my adult life."

Through this friendship attachment, he was forced to actually confront his sexual being for the first time. In many ways Nouwen's struggle with celibacy after years of celibate practice was like Merton's. Merton, however, had established his orientation and tested his sexuality prior to his monastic vocation. Unlike Merton and the young nurse, Nouwen's attachment was to a young man.

Although emotionally the conflict was identical to Merton's, the homosexual component added an additional layer of complexity and conflict to Nouwen's situation. The alternating currents of trauma and joy evoked by friendship—that such an experience might bring to an adolescent—were shattering to the man well into his fifth decade of life. He lacked the benefit of youth or the perspective of a non-celibate man of the same age might have brought to the situation.

Nouwen's commitment to the preservation of his celibacy made a rupture of this relationship the inescapable conclusion to his crisis. However, the experience of the separation from his friend was the most profound and painful of Nouwen's entire celibate career, which is to say, of his life.

Nouwen often wrote about loneliness. At last he could define the essence of celibate loneliness from anguished experience. Men—and women—who willingly choose to live without sexual gratification for a spiritual motive, cannot thereby simply and forever avoid confrontation with their sexual being, orientation, and emotions. Sexual experimentation and experience do not ensure sexual maturity or integration of sexual identity.

Celibacy—sexual deprivation—requires that a person develop alternate ways of refining the inevitable questions about his or her sexual orientation and identity. But sooner or later all the questions about one's sexuality need to be answered. That is a requirement for interior peace and freedom.

The proverbial dark night of the soul—a crisis of loneliness when one feels alienated from God and others—is an essential element in the process of celibate achievement. There is no way to avoid it. The crisis may come early in one's striving, in the middle, or late in the celibate process. The celibate crisis may come in waves that, at the time, seem unending and unmerciful. A person cannot precipitate it or predict its onset. The only possible preparation for the confrontation is celibacy itself. The way through the crisis is a thorny path that leads to freedom and peace.

The spiritual and emotional crisis involved in the pursuit of celibacy is only a dramatic expression of an inevitable reality that Nouwen wrote about when he spoke of the hole in the center of the soul, an emptiness that cannot be filled. We always require more and more, unendingly, from any human relationship, any friendship. Celibacy grapples with the reality of loneliness more directly, inevitably, and dramatically than any other sexual adjustment. Augustine expressed the human struggle as the quest of the "restless heart"; Dorothy Day called life and celibacy "the long loneliness." Whatever the term, religious celibacy—or profound spirituality—is not possible without confronting the inescapable deep loneliness within. Only by working through it can a person distinguish and then transmute it, to finally achieve the peace of aloneness that lies beyond.

PART III

THE PRACTICAL LIFE

One who is inimical to sex can never attain celibacy.
Sex is coal and celibacy the diamond.
The transformation of coal to diamond
Is like the transformation of sex to celibacy.

OSHO

Consolidation of one's sexual identity and the regulation of one's sexual behavior involve two different entities and distinct processes. Surely they are intimately related, but the task of putting them together always remains—to put sex in its place—whether that is in a celibate lifestyle or a sexually active adjustment. Integration of sexual identity does not automatically ensure that appropriate sexual behavior will follow. The indulgence or abstinence from certain sexual behaviors does not necessarily consolidate identity. But integration of identity and behavior makes adaptation easier.

It goes without saying that one is not sexually active in the abstract. Neither can one be celibate in a vacuum. Life has to be lived. That means that one has to work, sustain oneself, relate to others, and provide some useful service to humanity. A person does not have to be celibate, or married, or single to do any of those things, or all of them. We have to ask: what particular place does celibacy hold in our daily activities? And what do the tasks of daily life have to do with celibacy?

Pope John Paul II says: "Celibacy is to be regarded as an integral part of the priest's exterior and interior life, and not just as a longstanding ideal." Priesthood is not just a profession, a career, or a means of earning a living. "Rather, the clergy must see the priesthood as a vocation to selfless, loving service, embracing wholeheartedly the esteemed gift of celibacy and all that this involves."

Actually, the same statement should be made of married sexuality. Sex is a gift to be regarded as an integral part of a married person's exterior and interior life. Marriage is not a profession, or a means of earning a living. As many parents and lovers know, marriage is a vocation to selfless, loving service, embracing wholeheartedly sexual commitment and all that that involves.

Celibates need to be as persistently conscious of their celibacy as any sexually active person is of sexuality. The way to celibacy is found not by forgetting, but by awareness. Consciousness of one's own sexuality—and therefore celibacy—in all of its dimensions and permutations in one's life and work is the requisite path to celibate achievement.

The incorporation of celibacy into priestly—or any other—life is not just a matter of dedication to the selfless life and a willingness to perform loving service. It means fully grasping the sexual life in order to transcend sex. A person cannot free himself from sex by shutting his eyes. Sex will not vanish or relinquish its power through the act of ignoring it or pretending it is not there.

I have learned a great deal from the hundreds of case histories of priests and bishops who were in serious conflict because of celibate violations. In every case, celibacy was not integrated into their daily awareness. Many had "put sex aside" only to be overwhelmed by their underdeveloped nature. Many others maintained a double life, performing their professional duties even in an exemplary fashion, but having a fully sexual life in secret.

I am not talking about a rare, but understandable, sexual act. If we look at the model of Alcoholics Anonymous and their understanding of sobriety, I think we get a clearer picture of the struggle for celibacy. One is either sober or not. One is either living the program or not. And just as sobriety takes daily awareness and commitment to keep sober, one must sustain daily awareness and commitment to be celibate.

The clergy, by and large, do not take celibacy seriously. Their embrace is too secret, defensive, and too erratic to ensure daily consolidation. Without a doubt the clerical system has indulged in a lot of self-deception and denial by considering contradictions to celibacy merely as slips—sins to be easily forgiven—rather than signs of potentially serious maladaptation to a professed way of life. Hypocrisy is incompatible with any religious profession.

Celibacy can never be assumed of anyone. Sexuality is a part of every human; some sexual behavior is the ordinary expression of most humans. Celibacy has to be proved on a daily basis—primarily to oneself.

16

WORK AND SERVICE

Do you think you can eat bread
Without sweating to produce it?
Do you have a prerogative above
Nature's Law?

JOHN DONNE

Work has become a dirty word. It is the source of endless complaint. Work to many people is something we have to do so we can be free for the important things we really want to do. The dignity of work, the idea of proving ourselves in some tangible way, the satisfaction of accomplishment and self-mastery seem to have been absorbed and obscured by the bottom line. Many times work is evaluated by how much money it brings, and how much esteem it has in the eyes of others. Religion and churches are not immune from the culture of money and the measurement of success in dollars and prestige.

Have you ever been impressed with how deeply the idea of success, good health, and good fortune are equated with God's blessing? In some religious groups these are accepted as sure signs of God's favoritism and ratification of a person's goodness. The conundrum is as old as Job and as new as the latest TV ad or Sunday sermon. Some religious TV evangelists exhibit the extreme of this attitude. Their portrayal is easy to caricature. No one is immune from the virus of admiration (and envy) of the rich and famous.

Fascination with fame is rampant, and religious leaders can flaunt their power and popularity in epic, colorful religious displays and through pronouncements and public relations releases. Some of the hoopla can be justified and useful to the "selling" of noble ideals and attracting followers to good causes. But the image of grandeur and success are the ribbons of evangelization. The transformation of spirit is more tightly wrapped in action, often unseen, and in ordinary work—little glamour, but solid service.

Power is universally admired, sought after, treasured, and even worshiped as if it originates in the divine. The tendency to gravitate to the powerful, the famous, the wealthy—or even better—to be powerful, famous, or wealthy is so ubiquitous it is not questioned when religious people bask in the reflected light of worldly success or achieve it themselves. Power is like fire, capable of destroying the one who possesses it.

Some people "ooh and ah" when a person says he graduated from Harvard Law, Stanford, or the Ivy League. We tend to be impressed with the titles, Doctor, Reverend, Senator. A CEO who makes millions annually, a sports figure or movie star who merits frequent mention in the press all receive the same public awe as if these persons inhabit a different realm than the rest of us—where the rest of us would like to be.

If a person identifies himself or herself as a celibate, a certain amount of prestige or awe can be generated in some circles. The assumption resonates with the idea that such a person is special, strong, altruistic, dedicated, and holy. The ideal of celibacy does encompass all those goals and qualities. When that identification is coupled with institutional support, those assumptions can reach a mythical level. The reality of how celibacy is actually practiced gets obscured by the presupposition that people who call themselves celibate actually are what the Church holds up as ideal. But the ideal is the ribbon, the decoration. The assumption of celibacy serves as a detriment to the person who wants to achieve celibacy if he or she pretends it is a reality—a deserved aggrandizement—instead of a goal to be proved by work, service, and sacrifice.

Columnist and author William Cleary put the danger of clerical celibate identification succinctly: "Celibacy has become a kind of clerical garb. Celibacy creates the illusion of being superior. It requires one to act superior. Coupled with ordination to the priesthood it confers a superior feeling based on the massive illusion of being changed metaphysically—a priest forever, never again an ordinary human. Superiority enjoys its entitlement; it allows one to overpower others through orthodoxy, opulence, and sex."

A stance of superiority is diametrically opposed to the idea of celibate work and service. Service has lost its dignity along with work. We frequently refer to "service positions" when trying to identify work that we think is menial—as if professions are not meant to be service positions. Many times I am struck by the self-demeaning attitude manifested by some men and women who perform services we all need and should appreciate. For a time, I taught in a medical school. Twice a week I would get my lunch in the hospital cafeteria. The four people filling orders and working the cash register never looked any of the customers in the eye. Their conversations were restricted to each other. From my point of view, they were as important, noble, and as deserving of respect as any doctor or patient in the house. I felt cut off and outcast. Of course, if any of us looks down on our own work of service we will naturally demean others and isolate ourselves.

Paradoxically the same isolation and diminution of humanity results when anyone holds himself above others. The stance of superiority and entitlement is one of the serious occupational hazards of institutionalized celibate culture.

Many people who identify themselves as celibates do hold themselves as superior, even if they are not living celibately. They cling to the outmoded idea that they are on a preferred plane or living in a "higher state" than where others exist. They think that they deserve special treatment, that they merit special concessions, or that other people's money and time should be at their disposal, just because they are celibate. They claim that the honors are not for "them" but because of their "special role."

Celibacy is proved not by inclusion in some group or by public perception. Celibacy deserves no special consideration, nor admiration above any other way of loving and serving. A life of celibacy is freely chosen, just as marriage is. A person who calls himself celibate deserves no special recognition or admiration. Celibacy is proven by practice, by living it. The genuineness of celibacy will be demonstrated by the work and service it generates. "By their works you will know them."

People who value their work as service—whatever it is—equally intrigue me. The idea that a "professional" is superior to a farm laborer is not Christian. Chesterton said, "There is even a Christian way to learn the alphabet. That is not to look down on one who does not know it." We all need one another. Doctors need patients. Professors need students. In fact, healing can take place without doctors and learning without teachers. But it just works better if we realize how interdependent we are and do our work accordingly. Meditate a bit on all the people we need to live our daily lives, to do our work, and to deliver our necessary service; the grocer, the mechanic, the waitress, the deliveryman, the gardener, the receptionist, the painter, the postal worker, and so on. Which group could you afford to eliminate? There must be some reason why Christ identified himself as a carpenter, and most of his disciples were identified as fishermen. He was not a king with a court. He had no power except his service.

Better/worse higher/lower have no meaning in the Christian work ethic. The reason is that we are all one in Christ, and every work should be a service. Each of us has a place determined in part by circumstances beyond our control, but modified and enhanced by our motivation, knowledge of potential, opportunities, luck, and by other people.

In the Christian scheme of things, there is no higher or lower. We need to repeat this fact often and apply that reality daily—we are all one in Christ. The practical implications of believing in our equality are boundless for our transformation.

Celibacy, if practiced, does teach us this lesson, for we all have a sexual nature. Embracing our sexuality deeply, as celibacy demands, inevitably leads to humility—a rightful self-evaluation. It is impossible to imagine a person who practices religious celibacy as holding himself or herself outside the circle of human life. Celibacy is a confrontation with the fullness of one's humanity and all of its capacity for good and evil. This dimension is expressed differently by different individuals. Mother Teresa or Vincent de Paul could memorialize the experience when they considered a murderer, "There but for the grace of God go I."

Saint Paul, the primary Christian model for celibacy casts his ideas about celibacy in very different terms than prestige, power, or superiority. Celibacy is for service. And the work of the Gospel was not for self-aggrandizement, for lording it over others, or for personal fame or profit. He didn't deny that the "laborer is worthy of his hire" in the sense that ministers could sustain their basic needs by their preaching and ministry. But he refused to profit even in that way from his service. He worked, perhaps at sailmaking, to earn a living. No one could say he took financial advantage of his preaching.

The idea of our work being useful, even salvific for others and ourselves, has also lost fashion. Paradoxically, I hold that this lost focus is more true of clerical ministry than that of other professions and more prevalent now than in some former periods of the Church. The externals of faith and religion have superseded the spirit. Pretense triumphs over substance. What appears to be true is extolled over what is really true. Inspiring or juridical words substitute for actions.

No doubt some clergy and religious who profess celibacy do indeed work hard. But as a group they are, in the words of a psychiatrist friend Dr. Robert McAllister, "the most pampered and indulged" group of adults one can find. The built-in job security, living provisions, healthcare benefits, social advantages, freedom from familial responsibilities, and prestige accorded to a cleric or religious without regard to personal merit or productivity lays a foundation for expectation. Eugene Kennedy has called clerics "the last vestige of the landed gentry." Obedience, poverty, and chastity are promised as the price for institutional benefits. Only the person living within the system can judge how well poverty and chastity figure into the equation of his or her life. And these elements are connected. How genuine, or how much of a sham, are these elements in one's work and service?

Some people claim that they "work" better when they don't keep their promise of celibacy. "It's just sex." "Who does it hurt?" We can talk about those assertions and the problem of integrity later. For now, we have to recognize the essential links between poverty, celibacy, and service. One does not have to practice celibacy in order to preach, teach, heal, or perform any service well, or for that matter to be happy or successful. The question remains: What does celibate practice contribute to the quality and substance of the work to be performed?

The link between the value of celibacy, poverty, and the dignity of labor is not incidental. Let me put it as starkly and realistically as I have experienced it in my seventy years of life. One cannot achieve celibacy without valuing work as service over money and prestige.

My convictions about this were consolidated when I met Dorothy Day during my high-school years. I spent a summer on the Catholic Worker Farm in Upton, Massachusetts, in 1949. Day and her community embraced "voluntary poverty." Her attitude toward material things, her service to the poor, and her dedication to celibacy were part of the whole cloth of her existence.

She was converted to Christ from Communism, but she retained her sensitivity for the poor and her commitment to social justice, but transformed it. Her choice to serve the poor and fight for justice was now inflamed with the spirit of Christ. The quality of her service to the poor was marked by the clarity of her celibacy. Could she have fed and clothed the poor had she not been celibate? Certainly. What would the difference be had she not lived a celibate dedication? That is a question a person who wants to be celibate should ask—and decide for herself or himself.

Celibacy should not be a ticket to the benefits of clericalism. There is really no intrinsic prestige or honor connected to it. Celibacy practiced and lived is one powerful way of serving and loving others through our work. Celibacy lived inevitably engenders a deep appreciation of all people and all work.

17

HANDLING SUCCESS AND FAILURE

Repentance reaches fullness
When you are brought to gratitude
For your sins.

ANTHONY DE MELLO

It's here in all the pieces of my shame
That now I find myself again.
I yearn to belong to something, to be contained
In an all-embracing mind that sees me
As a single thing.

RAINER MARIA RILKE

What is a celibate failure? And just as importantly, what does it mean to succeed at celibacy? Those are not easy questions to ask, let alone answer. In several other places, I have written about celibate achievement, its characteristics, and how it looks (*Sex, Priests and Power*, New York: Brunner-Routledge, 1995). I have also addressed the various modes of celibate violations. Here I am proposing a collective examination of celibate conscience about success and failure. Let's zero in on the personal and practical struggles that confront us with ourselves.

The ideal of celibacy set before a cleric is awesome—perfect and perpetual chastity. Part of the confusion about celibate dedication versus the moral requirement for any ordinary layperson rests in the fact that the official Church teaching about sex states that every sexual thought, word, desire, and action outside marriage is mortally sinful for anybody. But the practical distinctions between sexual activity of one preparing for marriage and one dedicated to celibate chastity are not on the same plane or in the same order of activity. An identical sexual action, relationship, or violation is not equal for both.

One analogy may be telling a lie in casual conversation versus stating the same untruth under oath in a courtroom—same fact, different responsibilities, different effects. The first may be a sin, the latter is a crime.

Priests are used to being understanding, compassionate, and forgiving of people who come to them for counsel and confession when troubled, worried, or guilty over their sexual transgressions. But the problem of Christian sexual morality is deeper than pastoral compassion. Sexuality and Christian morality are more profound than reinforcing laws and intensifying "orthodoxy." Standard categories of sin and virtue, traditional interpretations of the distinctions between law (teaching) and pastoral practice, are not adequate to meet the intellectual and spiritual needs of people today. The understanding and practice of celibacy are vital for us and for future generations—all of us married, single, religious and clergy. We genuinely are on the edge of new era of understanding of human nature and unexplored dimensions of spirituality.

Early on in *On Human Nature* (Harvard University Press, 1978, p. 4), E. O. Wilson traces the path from molecular biology to mysticism: "In order to search for a new morality based on a more truthful definition of man, it is necessary to look inward to dissect the machinery of the mind and to retrace its evolutionary history."

That is a daunting challenge. In the heat of sexual passion, confusion, and temptation, the task of understanding the meaning and dynamics of sex and celibacy may seem distant and irrelevant. Understanding sex and celibacy, however, is eminently practical for social and spiritual life. The success of celibacy hangs in the balance.

In addition, the teaching of sexual reality and responsibility to Christians is intimately related to celibate honesty.

For me, the quest to understanding celibacy and sexuality from biology to mysticism has been worth a lifetime of effort and exploration. In 1991 my friend Henri Nouwen wrote a letter of encouragement. "I, personally, feel that you have a great vocation in this area....You have very important things to say and I have the feeling that rediscovering or reliving the mystical dimension of the sexual life may help you and me and all of us to grow to a reclaiming of live's (sic) sacredness." Encouragement from priests like Father Nouwen, Father Bernard Häring, and others has been essential to withstand the frustrations of investigating the delicate, dangerous, and emotionally laden dimensions of unexplored human behavior. Anyone striving to live celibacy will need to withstand similar obstacles.

A major source of resistance to any new understanding of sex and celibacy in the Catholic Church is the assumption that "everything is settled." That assumption is not true when it comes to practical life and decisions. Sexual moral doctrine has been cast in black and white. Any attempt at dialogue can be interpreted as an attack on orthodoxy, or worse, a corruption of morals. Of course, it is neither. A careful consideration of the practical execution of the parameters of law binding celibates will be helpful. Those legal parameters are "perfect and perpetual chastity."

The requirement of "perfection" is not only daunting, but also perhaps impossible. Do not take my word for it. Saint Jerome said: "For a religious to be perfect in this life is impossible; but for him not to strive after perfection is a crime."

As I have said earlier, celibacy is a process. It is dynamic. It is a part of life and meant to grow, develop, and flourish as life progresses. Does this view of celibacy as a process mean that one will make mistakes? Probably. Perfection in any area of human endeavor does not come immediately or automatically at the starting point when a person defines his or her intention. In striving for celibacy, it is good to remember the old saying, "The greatest enemy of the good is the perfect." The difficulty of being perfect should not discourage us from being good.

The probability of failure does not excuse one from responsibility for faults, mistakes, and bad decisions. Nor does the probability of failure give absolution from struggling to understand what elements, circumstances, and internal dispositions influenced the abandonment of celibate intent even briefly. In the end, noncelibate experience must be positively incorporated toward the goal of celibacy. Again, I recommend the dynamism of an Alcoholics Anonymous approach that is so coherent and consistent with the teaching of the Desert Fathers. Openness and radical truth about oneself are the keys to spiritual growth and self-control. Many people defeat themselves by keeping up pretenses even with themselves. Secrecy is the royal road to scandal.

One religious superior vigorously objected to the concept of celibacy that I laid out in the beginning of this book. He said "two or three failures in a year" does not constitute a negation of celibacy. Looking at sex and celibacy by the numbers is dangerous. It is also risky to view sexual behaviors as isolated acts—sins simply to be confessed and forgiven. According to such thinking, a man could impregnate three women in one year or abuse three minors during that time and still consider himself celibate. (Perhaps the priest was thinking of masturbation—an imperfection that can at times be compatible with celibate striving.)

Most people who remain celibate in name but not in practice don't usually decide all of a sudden that they will become sexually active. They slide into an act through naiveté or inexperience rather than through calculation or malice. At the very least, isolated mistakes do deserve the benefit of the doubt, but when act develops into practice, and practice results in a pattern or relationship, the integrity of celibacy no longer exists.

Denial, rationalization, avoidance—or whatever one calls lying to others and oneself—are more destructive of celibacy than the sexual drive itself. One cannot justify patterned sexual behavior with celibacy.

First, let's look at the range of possible sexual activity. Masturbation is the most commonly reported sexual activity of men and women who strive to be celibate. This activity is difficult to lump with the expanse of possible sexual activity. Although traditionally it has been categorized as a mortal sin, many moral theologians find that it rarely meets the criteria of a grave transgression. Psychologists and confessors often regard it closer to nature than to sin. This observation does not mean that a celibate can disregard its personal meaning, or neglect to take responsibility for it. The smart thing to do is to find the link between the behavior and the person's current state of mind and heart, stress and discouragement, and goals.

Any sexual activity that is criminal cannot by any stretch of the imagination be compatible with a celibate life. We have had to learn some painful lessons in the past decades from the widespread exposure of priests who sexually abuse minors. Church law—as well as civil law—has identified sex with minors as a crime. Since the first centuries the Church has legislated punishments against bishops, priests, and deacons who have sex with minors (Council of Elvira, A.D. 309), and consistent Church legislation demonstrates that abuse of minors by clergy is and has been a prominent, ongoing, and serious concern throughout the centuries. The most realistic estimate is that 8 percent of Catholic clergy involve themselves sexually with a minor at one time or another after they profess themselves as celibates. There can be no excuses for this behavior from anyone who wants to be celibate.

An overpowering sadness envelops anyone who studies this problem in the clergy and listens to denials and rationalization—at times even during sexual activity. "This is my way of showing God's love for you." "If God did not want you here with me he would not have sent you to me." "I am trying to give you a good education about sex." These and other similar statements are recorded in the depositions of hundreds of victims, some who were as young as eight years old when told these lies.

Priest abusers frequently protest that they did not think that they were doing anything wrong, they really "loved" the victim, they were trying to help. This misguided and culpably negligent logic defies reason and often borders on the absurd. "I simply gave the kids what they wanted" was the testimony of one priest who abused more than 150 minor boys. The statements of bishops who have blamed victims suffer from the same incongruous misunderstanding of human nature and celibacy. Surely, it ought to be expected that celibate ministers and teachers should be working diligently to protect, not harm, children. Who but clergy should lead the fight against abusive behavior in society and in the Church? Celibacy demands it.

In this cyber-age child pornography is available to anyone who has access to a computer. It goes without saying that pornography is incompatible with the practice of celibacy. Possessing child pornography is a violation of federal law. I have had the painful experience of seeing young priests sentenced to prison for having child pornography on their computers. A celibate simply cannot indulge in pornography. It is not a victimless crime. There are legitimate ways to educate oneself about sexuality. Child pornography is not one of them.

Sex with a married person is not compatible with celibate striving. Any sexual activity that imposes on a power differential between the partners is illegal and beyond noncelibate (sexual harassment). Clergy are given special trust if they claim to be celibate. They enjoy positions of spiritual power that invite people to share their vulnerability. Often, the very settings where people seek spiritual healing are turned into sites of exploitation—confession, spiritual direction, pastoral instruction, care of the ill, and so on. Such exploitation by trusted spiritual leaders in these settings is horrendous. It constitutes a betrayal and a distortion of nature with serious long-term damages to the victim.

Sexual pleasure and activity are complex because they are eminently detachable from relationships and love.

Reputable men and women have conducted secret heterosexual or homosexual affairs or indulged in a whole range of sexual paraphilias—cross-dressing, fetishism, voyeurism, compulsive masturbation, and so on—and still remain responsible parents, executives, and politicians. So it has long been with clergy.

Some Christian men and women who profess celibacy can and do have active sexual lives at the same time that they work productively and meritoriously. Witness the hundreds of priests who have unquestionably violated many, or even a few people; many parishioners continue to support the priest for his good services to the community.

With celibacy, it is not popular support that counts, but honesty and integrity. A person can conduct a secret sexual life separated from his or her public image, but not all secret sex is without severe consequences. Judy Thomas of the *Kansas City Star* did a survey of priests who died of AIDS. She reviewed the death certificates of priests between 1989 and 1998 and found that between two and four times as many priests died of AIDS-related causes as did men in the general population (*KCStar* 1/31–2/3/00). The assumption is that most of the infections were passed through anonymous sexual contacts.

Other men and women weary of the practice of celibacy, but unwilling to abandon the comforts and security of their public profession seek sexual comfort that is not illegal. Their activity can be with a man or woman for whom they have no professional responsibility. It is even understandable that a pressured cleric could turn to a hooker or hustler, bar-mate or erotic masseuse, for some secret comfort. One may be able to rationalize the behavior as either legal or nondestructive. Some go so far as to claim that their work and ministry is aided by such sexual activity.

That may be. But such activity, often tinged with genuine loving feelings, is not celibate. Those who want to be celibate must struggle at the deepest level of their being with the question: What does this action mean about my life, my goals, and me? Failure should not be denied. It must not be buried under a mound of guilt. Easy guilt and facile forgiveness perpetuates the cycle of failure.

Beliefs—that without exception all sexual pleasure is mortally sinful or sex acts are of little consequences—do not protect from failure or justify behavior. Rigid orthodoxy is not a substitute for responsible and honest behavior. People violate their stated beliefs all the time. Liberal or orthodox professions of faith are quite separate from what one does. Remember, I said earlier that the practice of celibacy is a personal and solitary journey. You may be able to find others, some in authority, who will cajole and condemn you for your celibate failures. You may be able to find those who will comfort you and easily forgive any transgression, encouraging you to see faults as separate acts. Neither is of help in determining your celibacy.

There is a significantly large group of clerics who literally opt out of celibate practice, but maintain their clerical status. In my lifetime, I have known, or known of, cardinals, archbishops, bishops, abbots, religious superiors, and priests who have sexual friendships and deep personal commitments with women or men that do not meet the common-sense definition of celibacy. This reality, although difficult to endure, should not deter one's determination to strive for and practice celibacy.

There is a fallacy that assumes that guilt keeps people from bad behavior. This belief is not true. Guilt does not ensure goodness or success. People—when they are who they want to be, and are what they say they are—constitute the reality of being and goodness.

Failure can only be mastered if one embraces it completely, accepts responsibility fully, and measures actions against "Who do I say I am?" One cannot wrap oneself in an ideal, no matter how exalted, and continue to pretend that it substitutes for or hides the reality of who one really is. Celibacy practices celibacy.

The popular writer Father Andrew Greeley calls priests "celibates." This statement is not accurate from an operational point of view. A priest may or may not be practicing celibacy. He argues that studies show that priests are among "the happiest men" in America and just as mature and capable of intimacy as comparable men of their age. These kinds of generalizations are really destructive of clerical celibacy because they skirt the real issues: what is celibacy and how do those who profess it practice it? Greeley's assertions say nothing about celibate failure or success.

Many men and women who set out to be celibate do achieve it. They are successful. But success, like heaven, is harder to talk about than failure and imperfection; the latter are ever with us and part of our practical day-to-day lives. Dante's *Divine Comedy* and Milton's *Paradise Lost* are but two examples that speak to my point. The eloquence of both poets reaches its apogee in their depiction of human struggle, pain, failure, and suffering already tested. The joys of heaven tend to be unimaginable, or as Saint Paul says, beyond words.

Celibacy must be established and won on a daily basis. This means that celibacy must cope with the joys and sorrows of existence, which no state in life can avoid. Some years ago a friend of mine, Peter Martin, wrote a book entitled *The Joys and Sorrows of Parenthood*. Many folks found it helpful because it was real, honest, and practical. Were I to offer one piece of advice to men and women who were beginning a celibate career I would suggest that they keep a personal journal about the joys and sorrows of celibacy as they experience them.

Such a journal would not proceed on the cliché that "virtue is its own reward." It would be a practical running account about one's work. The person accomplishing any work will mark it with his or her being and person. And work—any work—will mark the worker. Yes, there should be a celibate dimension to this interaction. Following closely the work in which one engages will tell a person a lot about herself or himself.

A journal would also be a record of one's prayer and development of interiority. That account could well be a complement to the daily prayer of consciousness that Father Frank O'Connor talks about in the Foreword to this book. Part of that prayer is a review of one's community or relationships. Relationships, knowing where they exist and consciousness of their meaning, are an essential consideration for successful celibacy.

Religious celibacy is of necessity an altruistic endeavor. Narcissism is the great destroyer of celibate intent and practice. The development of a sense of real service is essential to the success of celibacy. A record of one's sense of growth and service through the continuous struggle is useful as one matures through the process and the clarification of the personal meaning of a celibate life.

Naturally, a celibate man or woman has to take care of physical needs. Is there a "celibate" way to meet these needs? Yes, and without pretense or excuse.

In fact, this self care can be accomplished without compensating for the loss of sexual gratification by overdependence and indulgence in what are customarily called creature comforts. Poverty in the biblical sense does have a direct relationship to celibacy. It always has and always will. I was stumped by the biblical reference to the difficulty of a rich man—equal to that of a camel—getting through the eye of a needle (actually a narrow gate in Jerusalem). Studying celibacy taught me that the difficulty in following the narrow path also applies to anyone who claims superiority or carries "extra baggage." And celibacy is a narrow path. Keeping one's celibate a journal can help the celibate take stock of how one really satisfies his or her legitimate physical needs, and at the same time help to identify instances of carrying extra baggage or claims of superiority.

A journal will also be a check on how one is maintaining a balance in daily life. Ancient celibates severely deprived themselves of food, sleep, and emotional expression. Perhaps that is not the most effective way for modern celibates to ensure their success. Balance in one's daily life is a more certain way to ensure long-term success toward the goal. And it is not easy to keep a balanced existence. Maintaining balance is an ascetical discipline all its own. Instincts and circumstances easily combine to knock us off balance. Both become handy excuses to slip into neglect and disregard of our practice and goals. Keeping track of our balance is one of the surest safeguards of celibate practice.

Security—a certain amount of physical and certainly internal security—is needed to live a healthy life. Insecure feelings or circumstances can dispose us to poor decisions and regrettable behaviors. Insecurity can dispose us to overpowering loneliness. At times, the feelings of loss become indistinguishable from feelings of depression and hopelessness. Life tests the roots of our security; the inevitable dark nights of the soul find their refinement in the spiritual struggle of the celibate. Keeping close tabs on the sources and rhythms of our security is very practical in ensuring celibate practice.

Celibate practice requires order in one's life to maintain itself, and conversely celibate practice introduces order into existence. Order, regulation, is needed to counter the unpredictable and unruly nature of the sexual drive. Even if one has all the other elements in place to ensure practice, a person's journal can alert one to trends and tendencies that can spell danger if left unattended.

Learning and the love of it are a primary source of celibate support. I have been impressed with the journals of Thomas Merton. He made notes on his reading, his interests, about people he learned from, and with whom he corresponded. His journals take on a special tone because he was a writer, but they had meaning for his celibate existence regardless of their literary value. They formed a personal record that reflected the growth, development, and struggles of his mind and heart. Do not let the excuse that you lack literary talent or time to keep a journal from filling up the pages. Just like the prayer of consciousness, it is not the length of time that makes the difference. Consistency, awareness, and dedication to the celibate goal in a practical way on a daily basis is key to celibate success.

I have also observed that beauty, in any or all of its forms, fosters a person's celibacy. Music, art, literature, and so on, should be a part of the life of one who wants to be celibate. This appreciation for beauty is just part of the nature of celibacy. The ability to be renewed and sustained by creation tends to express itself in internal and external beautification of one's environment and life.

These then, in my experience, are the ten elements that support celibacy: work, prayer, community, service, proper attention to physical needs, balance, security, order, learning, and beauty. They deserve attention in the daily life of anyone who desires to live a celibate life. They can help one record the real joys and sorrows of celibacy. These are guideposts and aids through the maze of temptations and setbacks that may be encountered on the road to perfect and perpetual chastity.

18

WHO IS FAMILY
FOR THE CELIBATE?

A truly compassionate person
Is immersed in the spirit of the universe.
Security for self and others is in the Great Mother.
I will love others enough to let them go.
My peace will protect and nurture all.

ERICH FROMM

The simple and stark answer to the celibate's question "Who is my family?" is "You have no family. Christ is your only friend. The universe is your family." That comes straight from the Gospel (Mt 12:46–50). Certainly this attitude is an essential requirement of discipleship, and the Church holds that the tradition of celibacy is in intimate and essential concert with ministry. Others who wish to be celibate are absolved from the burdens of ministry and perhaps institutional restrictions and support, but they will find that the loneliness of celibacy has to be sustained and resolved in their lives just as much as any member of the clergy.

The seemingly harsh and unfeeling reality of the inevitable loneliness of celibacy merits some explanation. The experience of celibate loneliness is so profound it is difficult to describe adequately except in poetry and in almost mystical terms. Loneliness is an integral part of spiritual experience because those experiences touch the

Divine in ways beyond the physical, unbounded by time and space. Aloneness, the state beyond loneliness, is the readiness to receive spiritual closeness. Aloneness is the peace that makes one accessible to all creation. Traditionally this has been described as the awareness of God at all times and in all things.

A great deal has been written about the need and capacity that a celibate should have for intimacy. These considerations are useful but limited when they are presented as if legitimate celibate intimacy will obliterate the essential aloneness of a celibate commitment. It will not.

Nothing can ever take away from the human heart all trace of the desire for the other, the natural path that the Bible commands: "increase and multiply." The divine reflection, "it is not good for man (woman) to be alone" confronts men and women with a profound choice between Gospel "goods"—marriage or celibacy. Each is necessary in the scheme of salvation. Each path has its joys and sorrows. Each has its price and rewards. The price of marriage is commitment (sexual and spiritual) to one other person. The price of celibacy is the sexual and spiritual commitment to aloneness.

An eighty-five-year-old priest gave me the following meditation. He claimed he did not write it. He and I do not know where it came from. It is entitled "The Prayer of a Priest on a Sunday Night":

Tonight, Lord, I am alone.
Little by little the sounds in the church died down.
The people went away,
And I came home,
Alone.

I passed couples returning from strolls,
The movies disgorging laughing crowds,
Cafés filled with friendly groups enjoying
the day of rest.
I watched youngsters skating on the sidewalk.
Other people's children, who will never be my own.

Here I am alone. Silence troubles me.
Solitude oppresses me.

I am young.
I have a body made like everyone else's.
I have a heart meant for love.

I am celibate,
but it is hard.
It is tough to restrain a body
that would like to give itself to another.
It is difficult to love everyone and claim no one.
It is tiresome to shake a hand and not seek more closeness.

How can I inspire affection only directed to others?
How can I be a man only for others?
It is hard to be among others and not be like others,
Difficult to carry the burden of others,
Tiresome to sustain the feeble,
without the expectation of being carried or
having a claim on another's strength.

I accept the loneliness,
all the burdens of being alone.
I rededicate myself to celibacy.
It is my vocation, my way of being.
Celibacy is my way of loving and serving.

I am alone in communion with the universe.
I am at peace with being who I am,
and doing what I said I would do:
To be celibate.

This is as tender and accurate a description of the practical experience of celibacy as I have ever heard. Literature, especially novels
like Frank O'Connor's the *Edge of Sadness*, J. F. Power's *Mort*

D'Urban, James Joyce's and James T. Farrell's portraits of priests sketch the reality of celibate struggle. One might not think of them as very attractive advertisements for vocations. But they approach the truth.

The words of canon law are not an empty regulation: "Clerics are obliged to observe perfect and perpetual continence for the sake of the Kingdom of Heaven and therefore are obliged to observe celibacy, which is a special gift of God, by which sacred ministers can adhere more easily to Christ with an undivided heart and can more freely dedicate themselves to the service of God and humankind" (Canon 277).

Christian women and men who embrace celibacy are not bound by this law as priests are. But they share the same goals as clerics. They wish to be united to Christ with a close and personal bond. They, too, want to serve God and humanity in a meaningful way. They seek that pearl of great price—an undivided heart. They are recipients of a gift. That gift is a mysterious awareness that celibacy is the way they are called to live—a life of service without sex or family.

Celibacy is not meant to be a life without love or meaning. It is a gifted path that has to be freely accepted, even if there might be some grudging skirmishes in the process; but celibacy, like all gifts, has a price. The more fully paid the greater the benefits.

In my experience, men and women abandon the reality of celibate practice, even if only from time to time, more because of loneliness than for any other motive.

The collegial support and camaraderie of training programs are useful and important, but that time is comparable to the kindergarten and grade school of celibate living. It is not the grownup world of sexual and celibate challenge.

In training programs the real conflicts of life can only be prepared for in approximation. But all training programs are currently deficient and inadequate because they fail to deal with human sexual nature adequately. Even so, celibate skills, like battlefield skills, can be honed and tested only in the thick of combat.

Religious communities do provide some family-like structure for ongoing support. There is a reality to the brotherhood of the clergy, diocesan or order. But the support of brotherhood, however sweet, strong, and sustaining is not the same as the comfort of spouse, children, and grandchildren. That is what a celibate person has to give up.

But celibate dedication has its own rewards not wholly available to most married people. Reading the correspondence of the early Jesuits engrossed in their far-flung ministries, I am struck by how loving, uniting, and supportive of their work and their celibate resolve these men were of each other. The letters were genuine love letters. Love for each other, the whole Society, and their service to humanity and the Church. This is the service that celibacy is meant to make possible. This is the fraternal love modeled after Jesus and his apostles.

One, married or single, cannot love without running the risk of loneliness. No life can be lived entirely free of the experience of aloneness. The celibate is different. He or she of necessity says, "bring it on, aloneness is my path."

My own life's work has been to understand what celibacy is and what is the dynamic by which men and women arrive at their goal. I have also learned how and why some men and women fail in their attempt. One thing is certain, a person who practices celibacy has to go through loneliness and transform it into aloneness.

Most problems in practicing celibacy arise when a person tries to avoid loneliness. Loneliness is like fear: the more one tries to avoid it, the more power and force it accumulates. The more directly, resolutely, and honestly one confronts it, the more easily it gives way to the secrets that lie beneath it—the place where peace and meaning reside.

Some people who want to be celibate defeat themselves by trying to work, play, eat, drink, smoke, or socialize loneliness away. None of these options will work.

Celibacy is sexual deprivation. The physical longing to hold and be held by another—contact *ventrum a ventrum*—is so primal and so strong that only the gift of celibacy makes its sacrifice possible. All sorts of legitimate familial signs of affection are possible when one is anchored in a satisfactory marital relationship. Signs of fondness, warm hugs and kisses between siblings, close friends of either gender, or children, are more easily desexualized in the context of a life of one who enjoys legitimate sexual satisfaction. Difficult as it is to accept this fact means that the social signs of affection are of necessity somewhat restricted for the celibate.

Everyone has to pay attention to sexual boundaries—the celibate person more than anyone else. This boundary management does not mean that a celibate man or woman has to be stiff or distant. It does mean that a celibate has to pay close attention to physical boundaries and signs of affection (and movements of the heart) to a degree and in ways that others do not.

I wish that I had the talent to convey what I have experienced in reviewing hundreds of case histories—mostly of priests. Their celibate successes and failures are intimately tied to their ability to know themselves and respect boundaries or their disregard of those realities. The desire for family, so natural, good, and wholesome in itself, is often at the bottom of betrayals that have disastrous consequences. Celibacy is precisely not to have a family. Christ's statements about leaving everything and everyone to follow him must be thoughtfully absorbed by one who bases his or her celibate commitment on Jesus. His testimony that he had "no mother or brothers" was not empty metaphor. Simplistic and literal rejection of all relationships is also not in the spirit of the gospel. But the reality remains that no familial bonds can be counted on to fill the inevitable loss that celibacy demands. The hankering for a family is so strong and persistent that it constantly surfaces under many guises. Sexual temptations are often dressed as perfectly legitimate social, working, or ministerial contacts. The celibate person always maintains the responsibility of appropriate boundaries.

When a man or woman presents himself or herself as celibate, people expect that such a person is sexually safe. They have a right to presume that one who claims celibacy will have his or her sexual desires and behaviors in complete control. This confidence makes a celibate a natural recipient of trust. There is no question that people impose on that trust. The priest or nun, especially and even easily becomes the object of transferential love. Emotionally, they stand in for the father, mother, sister, brother, child, friend, lover—God—or of whomever the person may be unconsciously in need. Through all of this the celibate person must remain a person alone, without a family—a person beyond loneliness.

Naturally, I have examined the lives of many saints looking for the clues to their celibacy. In every case, I find a struggle with loneliness and the triumph of aloneness. I am fascinated with the life of Saint Vincent de Paul. There is a ten-year hiatus in his religious life when there is no recorded history of his activity. It is not necessary to solve the mystery of that time lapse to appreciate the wonder of his complete dedication to service of others without exception when he emerged from that veiled interval.

Saints—successful celibates—have much to teach. Each of them plunged into their loneliness—knowing it was a deprivation of family—and embraced it as a gift of nature. In so doing they transformed their lives because they emerged into the security of aloneness. Conceptualize transformation. Aloneness immersed in the spirit of the universe—secure in the Great Mother—produces the truly compassionate person. This unity, this embrace of all, is exactly what is on the other side of the pain, sacrifice, and self-knowledge of loneliness—the experience of the reality that we are all one.

The undivided heart is not a fiction. It is a reality of resolving the ambivalence of desire. A married person resolves this issue in the context of a sexual love relationship and the duties of family life. The core of Saint Paul's excitement over celibacy was his lived experience in which he found his undivided heart and the resolution of every ambivalence. His integrity was secured in aloneness free from family and from every sexual attachment. "We are all one in Jesus Christ—there is no longer Jew or Greek, slave nor free, male or female" (Gal 3: 28). We are all one: rich and poor, homeless and sheltered, smart and dumb, virgin and hooker, sick and healthy, powerful and powerless—we are all one. This oneness should become a reality for the sexually active Christian too, but the celibate is meant to bring the full weight of his or her talents to bear on the life of service without a family—alone with all of creation.

The reason poverty has always been closely allied with chastity—celibacy—is because there is an essential link between the two. If one is truly alone in the spiritual sense, his or her relationship with "things" also shifts. The irony of deprivation is that celibacy-lived is transformative. What seems to be all negative—the loss of personal sexual affection, dependency on comforting things, and the security of a place of one's own—are the building blocks of the imitation of Christ in the most fundamental sense. Through it all is freedom. The freedom of the children of God. The core of the celibate life is the experience of being alone, clinging to nothing, and feeling bereft of a sense of belonging—without a family, being no where. One's treasure is where one's heart is. The celibate must be free. The celibate is meant to be alive and a giver of life.

This is a hard doctrine. It always has been and always will be. To pretend differently is to deceive good people who seek a noble ideal and a worthy means of service.

Both the sexually active and the celibate Christian, learn from each other. Celibacy is not an easy, natural state nor is it a cheap grace. But we are all better and richer because of those who have had the courage to face up to loneliness in a radical way and grow through it into the fullness of aloneness without a family to call their own. The world is indebted to those who give themselves to a genuine celibate life and ministry.

19

LOVE AND LEARNING

Love is the only sane and satisfactory answer
to the problems of human existence.

ERICH FROMM

See God in all things, for God is in all things.
Every creature is full of God
And is a book about God.
Every creature is the word of God.
If I spent enough time with the smallest creature,
Even a caterpillar,
I would never have to prepare another sermon.
So full of God is every creature.

MEISTER ECKHART

This book has not talked much about love. That has been a conscious and purposeful decision. Talk is cheap, and talk about love is cutrate. It is applied across the board from hamburgers to movies, sex, and God with equal abandon. If you want to know exactly what I mean introduce the subject, "what is love?" to any group, social or professional, that you choose. Listen to what happens.

I have on my shelf a three-volume set entitled the *Nature of Love*. It is a worthy history of the idea from the Greeks to modern theories and scientific implications. A scholars' manual! Love, Spirit, God, mercy, and forgiveness are also words and ideas that abound in inspirational writing. For our purposes, talk of love must be backed up by real, practical, lived connections to our mind, heart, and actions, not just pious or comfortable feelings. As Pedro Arrupe says in his prayer (see Foreword, pp. 15–16), there is nothing more practical than falling in love with God.

Certainly, there are rock-solid comments about love in the Scripture. "God is love." No argument there. How does that become alive in daily life? "Greater love has no man than to lay down his life for another." That is a more stringent requirement, but possible. "Love others as I have loved you." That is a practical guide. Extremely demanding, but a standard for practical behavior nonetheless. It is not a problem to agree. It is a problem to live it out.

When I think about help in understanding and effecting these norms in my life I turn to a rather old book. *The Art of Loving* by Erich Fromm (Harper Collins, 1956, 2000) has become my favorite, because it is so practical and speaks to me in ways I can evaluate in my practical life. I recommend it to every reader. Although this book may not be to everyone's taste, but anyone pursuing celibacy should have some standard authors that help clarify the practical process of attaining truth and love in his or her life.

I am going to paraphrase Fromm. He begins by pointing out the necessity for the capacity to *give*. This turns most people's idea of love on its head, since we are so prone to think of love as getting. Fromm echoes Christ when he says, "What does one person give to another? He gives of himself, of the most precious he has, he gives his life." The records of priests who have failed at celibacy show that they lack this capacity. They cannot give because, in modern terms, they are narcissistic.

This is the most common character flaw of priests. Narcissim not only destroys celibacy, but also corrupts much of pastoral life. Narcissistic people can be attractive, clever, and productive, but their affective life is self-centered and self-serving. Many people suffer deeply when they are sacrificed on the altar of the narcissist's ego. These people dress up for themselves, welcome applause and wield power with grace and abandon. Narcissism really makes every love impossible, even love of God. If one cannot reach beyond self, if he or she is trapped in a hermetically sealed glass bubble, no real altruism, let alone love, is possible. They can see the outside world and even register the needs of others, but their actions are determined by how they will fare; their image, their interests, are paramount. These people are cripples when it comes to love. Their relationships are shadows. Their beauty is a portrait of Dorian Gray.

Fromm claims that four characteristics are present in every form of love: care, responsibility, respect, and knowledge. These four qualities are intertwined and interconnected. How could one claim to love another if he or she neglected to meet that person's needs? Parental care, pastoral care, medical care each imply a concern and a labor to serve the needs of someone. Care is work, labor for someone. Fromm uses God's interaction with Jonah to illustrate that "love and labor are inseparable." We love what and whom we work for and work for what and whom we love.

Responsibility in our context is not just duty, something we are required to do. It is the free act of being open and able to respond to the needs of another. Respect for another requires an acceptance of another person as they are. Jesus' interaction with the women and men who peopled the gospel is marked by inclusion. Sinners, lepers, harlots, tax collectors, the weak and impaired were received with equal respect and dignity. In fact, they seemed to have an advantage over the moneyed and more respectable citizens of his time. It was not that Jesus regarded them less; they were then, as some people are now, less accessible, more full of themselves, more self-confident and righteous than they have any right to be. Respect allows us to be free and allow others to be free. Respect is incompatible with domination or exploitation.

Some clergy, bishops, and priests who have abused minors claim that they loved the victim. Impossible, that is self-deception. Love and exploitation are radically incompatible on any level and in any relationship.

To know is to love. At least that is the only way we can explain the universal love of God. God knows each person perfectly. Respect and care become intertwined with the desire to know and encourage the process of knowing. Knowing is always incomplete, but is fundamentally connected with the challenge to love.

Self-knowledge and appropriate self-love are also tasks that need to be addressed in our quest to be lovers. Motherly love, brotherly love, love of God are models for learning and guides to sorting out genuine love, and certainly celibate love, from feelings, infatuations, and self-deceptions that have more incarnations than the snakes on Medusa's head.

Radical truth remains our touchstone. Daily attentiveness is our guide. Transforming love is our goal.

Learning is important for the celibate. And all knowledge of nature tells us something about the divine. Wide interests in life and continued curiosity have always been in the celibate tradition. Celibates should be scholars and wise people. The Hebrew tradition of the Rabbi-scholar has stayed more true to this priestly quality than modern ministers have. It doesn't make any difference what the interests are, just so they are engaging and gratifying. Literature, tapestries, and representations of the Last Judgment have been my intellectual passions.

Learning about celibacy should be an ongoing pursuit. If a reader thinks there is nothing to learn, he or she has missed the point of this book. The celibate, his or her daily life, work, people, challenges, plans, and goals are grist for the celibate mill.

Pope John Paul II, in 2004, when addressing some bishops about problems of sexual abuse in the American church, encouraged them to address "past mistakes and failures" and to learn from them. The knowledge gained, he said, "will contribute greatly to this work of reconciliation and renewal....Viewed with the eyes of faith, the present moment of difficulty is also a moment of hope." Learning is the salient word of the whole directive.

There is no question that the present moment of difficulty for the Catholic Church is one of the monumental crises that have marked its history and growth. At the center of this crisis are sexuality and celibacy. These are vibrant and living issues that affect the welfare and future of humanity. And they are as central to the growth of civilization and the development of morality at this time as were the conflicts that surrounded the Protestant Reformation and Galileo. We no longer fight and quibble over cosmology in the way our ancestors did. We agree the earth is round and travels around the sun. Grasping those seemingly simple facts about nature has revolutionized the way we see the world and ourselves and opened unimaginable ways to discover reality.

Human nature, and sex and celibacy by essential association, is the issue at the vortex of modern conflicts. Justice, war, reproduction, all rights, research from molecular biology to astrophysics cannot escape from their tie to human nature and their effect on it. We have carved out a narrow but vital slice of reality for consideration. Human nature and celibacy.

The Church identifies celibacy, the focus of our considerations, as a treasure and the jewel of the priesthood. This is why we turn to the priesthood for understanding and a model of celibate living for anyone who wishes to practice it. Human nature is our guide through the morass and confusion that engulf sex and celibacy.

Celibacy has been sold short. It has not really been seriously considered even in religious training programs. Critics will ask: "What is there to teach?" Even seminary educators dismiss the subject with minimal time and with as little fuss as possible, bowing mostly to critiques and reports that evaluate priests' maturity negatively.

Over the years, I have had chances to lecture on celibacy in seminaries. From feedback I have concluded that some of those efforts were useful, but over all I think I have failed. The system is against study and clarification. It is dangerous to tread the path Pope John Paul II mapped out: to face and learn from past mistakes and failures. But progress in any field from medicine to physics is the path through failure to success. And progress takes effort and learning.

Some years ago, I had the opportunity to construct and help teach a group of twelve seminarians for a three-week course. It was the only obligation any of them had for that period. Their requirements were to attend a one-hour daily lecture with the focus on *how to be celibate*. One two-hour group meeting each day focused on emotional responses led by a professional in bibliotherapy. The purpose of this segment was to sensitize each person to his inner responses within the unity and the safety of a text. This approach came from my experience of teaching several courses on the person of the priest utilizing novels to help seminarians understand this concept. The third element seemed to me the easiest. That was to spend an hour each day, divided into any convenient segments a person wanted, in reflection on celibacy. Not one person fulfilled that third requirement. That omission speaks powerfully about the inadequacy of any patchwork attempt to teach celibacy. It cannot be isolated into seminars or special add-on lectures. Learning celibacy must have an explicit and integral place in the seminary curriculum to be effective.

One time I was asked (by lawyers no less) to develop a syllabus to teach celibacy. I submitted a three-year, six-semester sequence for a theology program. My logic is that if celibacy is so necessary for the practice of the priesthood it merits equal billing with dogma and biblical sequences. This proposal seemed to be the only way the system can fully support the development of each priest as an expert in celibacy. More priests betray others, self, and their ministry through celibate violations than through doctrinal error.

Perhaps now the reader can more fully understand the remarks I made in the beginning of this book that a person who wants to be celibate has to count on herself or himself. I mean it. I fully realize that this way of looking at celibacy may strike some people as novel. It is the best I can do after forty-five years of devotion to the subject.

Some may wonder that I have said little about prayer. If people who choose to be celibate took seriously the words of Father O'Connor in the Foreword of this book, it would be sufficient, enough said. Prayer like love is frequently talked about, but more rarely developed and put into practice.

Above all, prayer is attentiveness. The prayer of consciousness is not the begging kind we are all so familiar with, one that asks for things, even the grace for celibacy. It is prayer that puts one in touch with reality: who one is, where one is, what one is doing, what one's relationships really are on a daily basis. That's where God will be found. The truth faced in the answers to these reflections is a prayer necessary for celibacy. Note that I said necessary, not optional.

Prayer, even celebration of the Eucharist, can become formulaic as far as celibacy goes. That prayer, along with psalms, the rosary, and other devotions, is compatible with a sexual life. Married people know that. Prayer is not antithetical or inimical to a sexual life. When one is married the thought of the partner permeates one's life and decisions. Work as well as prayer fit into the context of marriage and a sexual relationship.

Consciousness prayer or the *Examen* for the celibate is essentially incompatible with sexual activity. When one is celibate that very celibacy needs to permeate one's existence. Therefore one has a special dimension to attend to consistently. Many people fail at celibacy because this daily part is almost too easy, too simple. Believe me, consciousness of celibacy should be every bit as much a part of the everyday life of anyone who wants to practice it as daily ablutions.

Lived celibacy involves a transformation of the mind, heart, and body. It is a process as real as a caterpillar becoming a butterfly. It is unique and distinct from other ways of living. It is neither better nor worse, higher nor lower, than other ways of living. It does not mimic other reproductive transformations. If one wishes to practice celibacy, he or she will in the end find it natural, productive, and satisfying.

INDEX

ABOUT THE AUTHOR

Richard Sipe has spent his life searching for the origins, meanings and dynamics of religious celibacy. He spent eighteen years as a Benedictine monk and was trained to deal with the mental-health problems of priests and religious. He has been married for the past thirty-four years and has one son. As a monk, priest, and, later, a married man, he has taught in Catholic major seminaries and lectured at medical schools. He has served as a consultant and expert witness in over two hundred cases of sexual abuse of minors since 1992 and has written seven books on religious celibacy, including *Celibacy in Crisis* (2003), *Sex, Priests and Power* (Brunner/Routledge, 1995), and *Celibacy: A Way of Living, Loving, and Serving* (Liguori Publications, 1996).